Psychology of OFFICIATING

Robert S. Weinberg, PhD
Peggy A. Richardson, PhD
University of North Texas

Leisure Press
Champaign, Illinois

Dedication

To my family, for always being there when I need them.

R.S.W.

Library of Congress Cataloging-in-Publication Data

Weinberg, Robert S. (Robert Stephen)
   Psychology of officiating / by Robert S. Weinberg, Peggy A.
Richardson
      p.   cm.
   Includes bibliographical references.
   ISBN 0-88011-400-2
   1. Sports officiating--Psychological aspects. I. Richardson,
Peggy A., 1938-   . II. Title.
GV735.W45   1990
796--dc20   90-31893
                                                         CIP

ISBN: 0-88011-400-2

Developmental Editor: Ted Miller
Copyeditor: Claire Mount
Assistant Editors: Julia Anderson and
            Robert King
Proofreader: Phaedra Hise Hargis
Production Director: Ernie Noa
Typesetter: Brad Colson
Text Design: Keith Blomberg
Text Layout: Kimberlie Henris

Cover Design: Jack Davis
Cover Photo: Bill Straus © 1987
Illustrations: Artwork created at the Center
            for Instructional Services,
            University of North Texas by
            Thomas Vasquez, Michele
            Simmons, Mark Allen, and
            Mary Nash
Printer: Braun-Brumfield

Printed in the United States of America

10 9 8 7 6 5 4 3 2 1

Leisure Press
A Division of Human Kinetics Publishers, Inc.
Box 5076, Champaign, IL 61825-5076
1-800-747-4457

Contents

Preface

Officiating can be challenging, exciting, and rewarding. On the other hand, officials can also feel frustrated, abused, and unappreciated. Whether you experience the positive or the negative rests on your mental approach to officiating. Most officiating books and instructional camps emphasize the importance of positioning, mechanics, and knowledge of the rules. Yet top officials identify confidence, judgment, rapport, and decisiveness as the qualities most essential, though more difficult to learn, for successful officiating.

That's where the idea for *Psychology of Officiating* began: It became clear to us that psychological factors were the most critical, yet most tenuous, aspect of officiating. Players, coaches, fans, and the media may assume that officials can act and think like robots, but anyone who has officiated knows that nothing could be farther from the truth. Officials face as much pressure and emotion as do athletes and coaches.

Many officials know all the rules, use proper mechanics, and are technically skilled. What separates the best officials from the rest of the pack is psychological skills, which few officials take time to develop.

As former officials, we have worked a variety of men's and women's sports, including basketball, football, tennis, soccer, baseball, track and field, and volleyball at levels of competition ranging from youth league to college. We have known the pressures and made the split-second decisions required of officials. And we have sometimes fallen prey to the excessive demands of officiating. We are also both formally trained in the psychology of sport. Our practical officiating experience, our academic training, and our discussions with many other officials have convinced us of the need for this book.

Our major objectives for the *Psychology of Officiating* are these:

1. To establish the importance of psychological training and motivate you to begin a systematic program of your own
2. To describe the qualities and psychological skills of top officials
3. To discuss the psychological skills—relaxation, concentration, imagery, confidence, communication, goal-setting—that will help you reach your full officiating potential
4. To inform you of the specific techniques, strategies, and programs that will develop your psychological skills
5. To demonstrate that effective psychological skills will bring you both better performance and greater enjoyment as an official

Psychology of Officiating is based on both research and experience. Much of the data comes straight from studies of officials, and many of the psychological principles described were developed with other sport participants. We also interviewed many officials and have incorporated their ideas and insights about the mental side of successful officiating.

Part I of the book is concerned with getting you ready to officiate. Chapter 1 discusses the qualities consistently found among top officials, including confidence, rapport, decisiveness, judgment, integrity, focused concentration, and motivation. All of these qualities are in fact psychological skills that you can learn through practice. The challenge is to take the necessary time to develop such skills—not only to become a better official, but also to better enjoy your officiating experience.

Chapter 2 describes how to best prepare to officiate. Officials, like athletes and coaches, need to mentally prepare for each competition. We offer suggestions and strategies for getting ready, and we point out how the psychological skills discussed later in the book help you prepare for assignments.

In Part II we discuss the importance of getting along with players and coaches, beginning with good communication (chapter 3). Communicating effectively is not as easy as it might seem and requires listening as well as talking. Whether you're facing an irate coach, working with an associate official, or talking with an administrator before a game, effective communication is critical.

Self-confidence also helps officials communicate effectively, and we focus on developing this important attribute in chapter 4. Confidence is a building block of effective officiating—it affects almost everything you do. A confident official acts decisively and is in control of what's happening on the court or field. We discuss characteristics of confident officials, the relationship of confidence and performance, and techniques for enhancing confidence.

In Part III we address the emotional aspects of officiating. Chapter 5 suggests how to stay motivated as an official. It's tough to deal with the criticism and negative feedback that officials often receive; but setting specific goals for yourself can help maintain your desire and motivation. Simply setting goals, though, is not the answer; we present specific principles and strategies to help you use goals most effectively.

It is important to stay motivated and be pumped up for an assignment, but too much emotion can be detrimental. In chapter 6 we discuss the role that anxiety can play in an official's performance. First we present potential sources of anxiety and discuss how excess anxiety can affect you physically and psychologically. Then we describe and illustrate the relationship between anxiety and performance and identify relaxation techniques that can help you stay calm and in control under pressure.

Another key aspect of effective officiating is staying focused on the action. Effective focus of attention can help your decision making and improve your judgment. In Part IV we take a closer look at how officials can become better focused. In chapter 7 we discuss the concept of concentration, noting the unique attentional problems that officials face. We outline a variety of at-home and on-site strategies and techniques to improve your concentration.

An exciting technique that can help you concentrate, enhance your confidence, and reduce your anxiety is described in chapter 8. Imagery, which involves visualizing yourself performing, is particularly important for effective officiating. Because officials have few chances to physically practice their skills, mental imagery is a great way to prepare for a game. We present a step-by-step approach for implementing your own imagery training program, including exercises to use at home, before an assignment, or during breaks in the action.

Developing the psychological skills presented in Parts I through IV will help you become better at officiating and enjoy it more. Part V, "Staying With It," suggests ways to continue to enjoy officiating. Enjoyment is particularly important to officials because they so often get negative comments from coaches, athletes, fans, and the media. In chapter 9 we address the issue of burnout, which unfortunately strikes many officials. We define burnout, describe its stages, identify its contributors, and suggest how to prevent it.

Chapters 1 through 8 should have fully prepared you to deal effectively with most situations that arise during athletic contests. But outside-of-the-game influences can affect officials psychologically, including situations involving gambling, drugs, and legal matters. Therefore, you must know much more than just how to officiate a game. We address these important issues in chapter 10 and demonstrate how, if left unattended, such "outside" factors can have a significant psychological impact on your officiating.

By starting this book you have demonstrated your interest in becoming a better official. We hope that the skills you learn here will help you achieve your goal. Good luck!

Acknowledgments

We wish to thank all of the officials who graciously gave time to share with us their thoughts and feelings from their officiating experiences. Their comments were invaluable in conceptualizing and writing this book.

PART I

Getting Ready

Psychological Qualities of a Good Official

1

The game ended more than a hour ago. You no longer need to be extremely alert or prove yourself to the players, coaches, and fans. You feel drained physically and emotionally. So you sit back with a cool drink, put your feet up, and try to relax. But for some reason you can't unwind.

Your mind is replaying every call you made. You wonder what the members of the officiating crew think about your performance. You worry that you may have blown some calls, and you can still hear the criticisms of spectators ringing in your ears. Then you remind yourself to "leave the game on the field"—and you try. You tell yourself "I was prepared for the game"; "I worked well with other officials"; and "Overall, I did a good job." Yet the lingering self-doubt persists despite your efforts to toss it aside.

These conflicting postgame thoughts are not uncommon. All types of officials, whether voluntary or professional, must deal with them. They occur when you are a part of a large officiating group for football, volleyball, or tennis or when you work in smaller officiating teams for basketball, ice hockey, or wrestling. If you have officiated a sport recently, these disturbing thoughts are probably all too familiar to you.

THE OFFICIAL'S ROLE

Why do officials experience this inner turmoil? Much of it is simply a consequence of their unique role. After athletes and coaches, officials are the third dimension of athletic contests; yet officials perform one of sport's most difficult tasks. Good officiating facilitates the sport event, ensuring that the outcome is dependent upon the skills and tactics of the players. Poor officiating detracts from the contest and decreases the enjoyment of the game for players, coaches, and fans. The work of game officials is open to public scrutiny, and they are often discussed and publicized because of their mistakes. In contrast, when a game goes smoothly, few people ever notice the officials.

On what basis, then, should officials judge themselves or be judged? Their primary job is to ensure that a contest progresses according to the rules while interfering as little as possible.

More specifically, officials must be committed to fulfilling four major responsibilities:

1. See that the event proceeds within the context of the rules of the game.
2. Interfere as little as possible, never seeking to become the focus of attention.
3. Set and maintain an atmosphere for the enjoyment of the contest.
4. Show concern for the athletes.

MENTAL-PHYSICAL DEMANDS OF OFFICIATING

A strong relationship exists between the psychological skills and the physical performance of officials. Therefore, a referee's success or failure depends on his or her physical abilities (e.g., conditioning for the demands of a particular sport, techniques and mechanics, visual skills) and mental abilities (e.g., confidence, concentration, emotional control).

This relationship between the physical and psychological aspects of officiating is an interesting one. Officials most often talk about the importance of mental, rather than physical, skills in performing their difficult tasks—making the unpopular call, not letting the game get out of hand, staying cool, and not becoming rattled. In fact, veteran officials claim that managing psychological skills accounts for 50%-70%

of an official's success. Similarly, supervisors of officials in various professional sports (e.g., Art McNally, National Football League; Ed Vargo, National League baseball; L.R. Nelson, tennis), who assign and evaluate the work of referees and umpires, emphasize consistency, fairness, mental toughness, quick and accurate decision making, and calmness as the most important assets for good officials. Without question, sports such as tennis, track, and volleyball also place a premium on an official's mental skills. Other sports, however, like lacrosse and basketball, require officials to be both physically and mentally capable.

Thus it seems strange that training camps and clinics emphasize physical techniques, interpretation of rules, proper attire, and written and practical tests. If officials and supervisors agree that the mental aspect of officiating is critical to one's success, why is so little time and emphasis placed on developing and practicing psychological skills? A major reason is the misconception that psychological skills are innate: Either you have them, or you don't. In fact, just as physical skills can be honed, so too can psychological skills. Effective officials are not born with a complete set of psychological skills. Rather, their ability to concentrate, relax under pressure, maintain confidence, and relate to other members of the officiating team is systematically and repeatedly practiced. And because these qualities are indeed skills, they will dissipate just as physical skills do if not nurtured.

It appears, then, that a certain combination of physical *and* mental skills is necessary to become a superior official. Just what that combination is may become clearer as we discuss the most important qualities of a good official.

QUALITIES OF A GOOD OFFICIAL

Although officiating involves technical knowledge, there is definitely an art to being an effective referee. And the artistry displayed by an official in the competitive arena depends, in large part, on his or her personal qualities.

You might assume that these important officiating attributes have been identified and widely used as the criteria in evaluating officials. But if 100 different sports officiating experts submitted their own lists and rankings of essential qualities for an official, you could expect 100 different listings and dissimilar rankings. So we will not attempt to rank-order the qualities of a competent official nor try to provide an exhaustive list of these essential qualities.

Rather, based on the latest research findings, we summarize the characteristics top officials have in common.

- Consistency
- Rapport
- Decisiveness
- Poise
- Integrity
- Judgment
- Confidence
- Enjoyment/Motivation

After we describe these qualities, we then briefly discuss how they relate to specific psychological skills and the techniques used to develop these skills.

Consistency

Players and coaches expect officials to be consistent: Their decisions should be the same in identical or similar circumstances, and they should apply the rules equally to both opponents. Inconsistency in officiating is frequently criticized by—and upsetting to—coaches and players.

Officials themselves recognize the importance of consistency in their work. A recent study of basketball officials, for example, found that

73% of the sample agreed with the statement "I believe that consistency in one's officiating is more important than following the rules to the letter."[1]

Problems of Inconsistency

Experience has shown that a lack of consistency creates these and other problems:

- Players are always guessing what is allowed and what is not.
- Coaches become frustrated and less trusting of officials' competence.
- Officials try to "even up" calls, thereby punishing a team or athlete for previous officiating errors.

Players simply don't know what to expect when an official vacillates in decision making. If an official ignores a foul one time but then calls a foul for the same behavior later in the game, athletes and coaches become confused. This uncertainty often results in anxiety, frustration, anger, and eventually some negative physical behavior by those who perceive they are being cheated.

One of the greatest threats to consistency is an official's tendency to even things up. When asked, "Do you feel officials try to balance up a call when they have made a bad call against a team?", 77% of the officials responding agreed.[2] At first glance, this may seem like the fair thing to do. However, attempting to even things up only worsens matters by marring the game with deliberately made incorrect calls.

Achieving Consistency

True consistency results, not from attempting to even up calls, but from applying a uniform rule interpretation to each separate competitive action. No two competitive situations are exactly alike; it is up to the official to apply this uniform interpretation across the board. This ensures that the official's decisions will be viewed as consistent and fair. In essence, proper judgment and interpretation are the main sources of consistency.

This within-game consistency, which involves uniform interpretation of the rules in a single contest, is critical for effective officiating. However, an official's between-game consistency is just as important. That is, a good official applies the rules correctly and similarly game in and game out.

Achieving the consistency necessary to officiate at a high level requires two capacities. The first involves demonstrating good technique, knowing the rules, and exhibiting the qualities previously described. Many officials are inconsistent simply because they have not sufficiently mastered rule interpretations, basic positioning, and sport-specific officiating techniques. You must shore up your deficiencies in these areas before you can achieve consistency in your officiating. The second requirement for achieving a high level of officiating consistency involves your mental and emotional skills. Consistent officiating requires a stable mental state. Peaks and valleys in performance are often directly related to psychological inconsistencies. The ability to get in the proper psychological frame of mind and maintain it throughout the contest is critical to being an effective official.

Rapport

Rapport is the quality of relating effectively to others. A good rapport with others is desirable in any line of human endeavor and perhaps even more important in officiating. Officials must try to establish good rapport with both coaches and players. As an official, you are not trying to win a popularity contest, but you are not trying to make enemies either. The key to establishing a good rapport is effective communication. If you communicate effectively with athletes and coaches, they will more likely cooperate with you and less often question your decisions. We discuss the principles of effective communication in chapter 3.

Officials also can improve rapport by treating players and coaches with courtesy and respect. They should expect the same treatment in return from coaches and athletes. Although you should be friendly when officiating, you also need to maintain a proper distance from the competitors to dispel any doubt of your nonpartisan position. Be approachable and willing to listen to questions and complaints, but don't allow participants to interrupt the flow of the game with continued questioning. Avoid long debates by restarting the contest as soon as possible.

Decisiveness

An official's decisions should occur simultaneously with the action observed, or as soon thereafter as possible. This does not mean that you should make all calls without hesitation. You might need to take a slight pause to comprehend what you have just seen. But too long of a pause gives the athletes and coaches the impression of uncertainty, and they are much more likely to question a delayed call.

Judgment calls are not subject to formal protest. Thus, you can often avoid controversy by making quick and decisive rulings. And the closer the decision, the more important decisiveness becomes.

For example, a football official must make a definitive call and signal whether a ballcarrier struggling to get over the goal line has made a touchdown. Hesitation will only bring on questions and controversy. So clear, decisive action is imperative. Therefore when making such a call, an official must give the *impression* of being absolutely certain of what he or she saw.

Poise

Sport competition is generally exciting, and the action is often fast paced and rapidly changing. In addition, because of the importance that people in our society place on sports, it is not unusual for emotions and tensions of athletes, coaches, and spectators to run high, especially during the initial and latter stages of a competition.

An official must remain calm and poised, regardless of what is happening. Although you cannot necessarily control the emotions of others, you are expected to be in control of your emotions no matter what the circumstances.

In our interviews with officials, they consistently reported performing better when they were able to stay relaxed and calm. The ability to stay relaxed is extremely important for officials because more often than not they are under pressure from coaches, players, and fans. No matter how good you are at officiating, you will always make 50% of the coaches, players, and fans unhappy. Yet many officials try to please everyone. Such an approach is futile and detrimental. Putting pressure on yourself to make all the "right" calls will only increase your chances of burning out and becoming too self-critical.

Ron Luciano, a former major league baseball umpire, described in his book *The Umpire Strikes Back* how he benefited from advice he received about relaxing at the beginning of his career:

> I was trying too hard to run the whole show, said Barney Deary, a minor league supervisor of umpires. Let the other umpire handle his own problems, he said. I've watched you work, you've got enough of your own. We talked for a long time and he turned me around. Baseball's a great game, he said, but you're not enjoying it at all. Just relax and have fun out there. I took his advice and began easing up a bit.[3]

Part of being relaxed is not being afraid to make mistakes, disappoint people, or lose control. When officials describe their best performances, they recall not being afraid of blowing a call or being criticized by coaches and players. Instead, they reported feeling calm and quiet inside. When the mind is not preoccupied with the negative consequences of failure, it can focus on the task at hand.

Officials must maintain self-control at all times, especially during moments of high tension, when fights, injuries, fouls, and violent outbursts are more likely to occur. An official who remains poised and in control, while asserting authority and leadership, keeps such critical situations from resulting in an ugly incident. During tense moments, your gestures and movements should become more deliberate whenever possible. A certain amount of excitement is normal when you officiate, but it is important to keep your emotions and actions under control, never allowing them to jeopardize your effectiveness as an official.

Integrity

Integrity refers to calling a game in an unbiased, honest manner, regardless of the reactions of players, coaches, or spectators; the time remaining; the score; previous calls; or any other potential sources of influence. The best safeguard for maintaining your integrity is couched in the adage, "Call 'em as you see 'em."

It is extremely important to protect your integrity both on and off the playing field. Although you probably are aware of your responsibilities while officiating, you should be equally concerned about maintaining others' respect for your integrity off the field. This includes never airing your opinions about players and teams you might officiate in the future and never wagering, no matter how small the bet, on the outcome of any game you might officiate. Finally, you reveal your personal integrity by the officiating assignments you turn down. Never accept an assignment that might compromise your values, such as when a family member or close friend is involved as either a coach or a player.

Judgment

Good judgment begins with a thorough and complete understanding of the rules and regulations governing a particular sport. Once established, rule knowledge can serve as a guide for determining the legality of play. Then, sound judgment gained through experience will allow you to meet the demands of a variety of officiating situations. The official who continues to study the rules and applies officiating experiences toward personal improvement will likely become competent. You must repeatedly practice officiating to develop good judgment, just as an athlete must practice techniques to develop requisite physical skills.

When officials describe instances when they made good judgments, they invariably report that they were

- totally focused on the game, match, or event;
- unaware of distractions or able to effectively block them out; and
- unconcerned about previous calls and the subsequent reactions from those involved.

Good officials know that irrelevant thoughts detract from their effectiveness. One lapse in concentration can lead to a bad decision that spells the difference between who wins and who loses a competition. Many sporting events last 2 to 3 hours, so it is not an easy task to stay totally focused at all times. Fortunately, concentration is a skill that can be practiced and strengthened. Chapter 7 describes how to improve your concentration skills.

Confidence

Competent officials have confidence in themselves and their abilities. This self-confidence transcends any particular game or situation.

Confident officials remain in control during adversity. That doesn't mean that they experience no feelings of self-doubt, but they don't lose confidence in themselves just because they made a bad call or experienced other setbacks. Every official has games that he or she would rather forget, but confident officials don't let that undermine their genuine belief that they are good at what they do. Quotes from two veteran officials highlight the central role that confidence plays in effective officiating. A male high school basketball official told us:

> If you are not confident in yourself you might as well not show up. Coaches and players will quickly notice an official who lacks confidence in his or her calls and try to take advantage of the situation. I always try to convey a confident attitude and approach to my officiating. Without confidence in yourself, it is hard to get the respect of the players, coaches, and fans.

A female high school volleyball official concurred, stating that

> the difference between feeling confident when you're officiating and not feeling confident is that you don't hesitate when making close, critical calls and never second-guess yourself. You just go ahead and make your calls, knowing you are doing your best.

Although confidence can certainly be elusive, a successful official maintains a positive attitude regardless of the circumstances. Such officials are not concerned with events beyond their control; rather, they are confident that they will perform to the best of their abilities. If you go into an assignment expecting to perform poorly and not believing in yourself, you are setting yourself up for a long game. Because confidence is so crucial to successful officiating, it is discussed at length in chapter 4.

Enjoyment/Motivation

Top officials enjoy their job immensely. This sense of enjoyment and fun is strongly tied to a positive mental attitude and feelings of energy. Good officiating requires a lot of hard work, dedication, and practice. All of these stem from a high level of motivation, which is closely tied to enjoyment. If an official's enjoyment for officiating diminishes, he or she will lack the motivation to practice and work hard at the job. The common theme among officials who have burned out is that they have lost their enjoyment for officiating because of the intense pressures placed on them and the lack of appreciation for their efforts.

This lack of fun and motivation is captured by the following quote from a high school and college football official:

> I used to look forward to getting up in the morning on the day of a game I was going to officiate. I couldn't wait for the game

to start, as I enjoyed the experience of being involved in the action. But as time went on it became more and more difficult for me to get motivated to officiate even when it was a big game. I'm not sure if it was all the abuse I took over the years from players, coaches, and fans or just the boredom of doing the same thing over and over again. Whatever the reason, I just lost my enthusiasm. And when officiating wasn't fun anymore it really told me it was time to get out.

DEVELOPING PSYCHOLOGICAL SKILLS

Thus far we have attempted to demonstrate that being a good official requires not only knowledge of the rules of the sport but also a certain set of personal qualities. When you achieve the right mental state, your officiating will more consistently approach your potential. The key is optimally developing your psychological skills. The better you learn how to achieve these skills, the more likely you will be to realize your potential as an official.

For example, establishing rapport with coaches, players, and fans requires the development of communication skills. Learning to express yourself effectively, being a good listener, and facilitating cooperation are all parts of good communication.

Poise is related to the psychological skill of relaxation. Staying relaxed and calm, especially at critical times during a game, is an important psychological skill for officials. Dealing with the pressures of fans, players, coaches, and the media requires the ability to remain mentally and physically relaxed. This skill can be learned through relaxation techniques such as progressive relaxation, controlled breathing, and positive self-talk.

Decisiveness requires good concentration skills and proper attentional focus. Officials must stay focused on the action and not become distracted. Using attentional triggers, practicing eye control, and staying focused on the present are just some ways to help maintain the proper attentional focus throughout a contest.

The point is, the qualities that good officials possess are really psychological skills that can be practiced and learned. Unfortunately, as noted earlier, the typical training of most officials emphasizes physical techniques. But the skills that distinguish the best officials from others are mental, not physical. The good news for you is that techniques exist that can help you learn these important mental skills.

The remainder of the book focuses on helping you develop the psychological skills important for successful officiating:

- Communication
- Confidence

- Motivation
- Relaxation
- Concentration
- Imagery

In the chapter devoted to each skill, we first present basic information concerning the psychological skill and then discuss specific techniques, strategies, and exercises to help you enhance your use of the skill when you officiate. The goal is to provide you with specific, action-oriented instructions so you can practice, develop, and use the skills on the job.

Developing these psychological skills will take some effort on your part. But you have already demonstrated your commitment to improving just by taking the time to read this book. And, as you continue reading, you'll learn how to develop your psychological skills to the point where you can control your mental and emotional states, rather than having them control you.

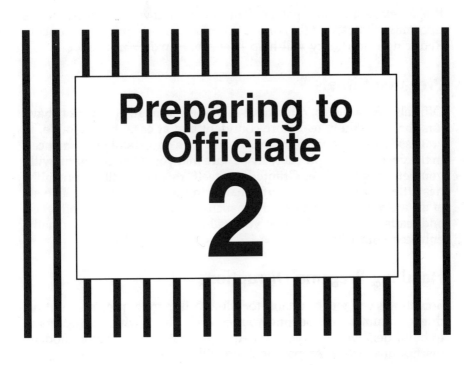

Preparing to Officiate

2

Peak officiating doesn't just happen. It takes more than good intentions to perform well during the contest. Reaching your performance potential is often a direct result of pregame preparation. Although each official will have to develop a pregame routine that best suits his or her personality and sport, this chapter presents some general guidelines for effective pregame preparation.

PREGAME PREPARATION

Your pregame preparation should include a consistent, reliable routine that primes you for the physical and mental demands of the contest. This routine includes such physical components as conditioning, sleep, and diet. Psychological or mental preparation involves concentration, self-talk, and imagery. The mental skills are discussed in detail in later chapters.

Benefits of Pregame Routines

Pregame routines (a) organize your time so that you can focus on the upcoming contest and (b) remove uncertainty from your environment. Reducing uncertainty will help keep your anxiety in check.

Pregame Rituals

Officials, like athletes, often have seemingly strange pre-event behaviors that help them feel more confident and at ease. For example, if you associate a certain good-luck charm with successful performances in the past, you will probably make sure that you have the charm with you before each game. Granted, in itself, this superstition probably has little to do with your performance in the game. But you, like all of us, are a creature of habit; and if such behavior gives you confidence and leads you to believe that you will perform well, it may actually enhance your officiating.

Handling Pregame Disruptions

Sometimes you will be unable to follow your regular pregame routine due to circumstances beyond your control. That's why it's important to build flexibility into your schedule so that you can accommodate disruptions in your preparation and still officiate well. Becoming too dependent on a specific routine prevents you from officiating well under unusual conditions. Periodically officiating a scrimmage or pre-season game without the use of your routine ensures that you can be flexible during more important contests.

Whatever pregame agenda you choose, your objective should be to develop a routine that is *ideal for you* and follow it. The remainder of this chapter offers suggestions and guidelines for establishing a routine that maximizes your officiating performance. However, because this book focuses on the importance of psychological skills, we only briefly describe the physical concerns before examining in depth the mental aspects of game preparation.

PHYSICAL PREPARATION

Officials are subject to great physical demands for extended periods of time. But different sports require different degrees of physical conditioning. Judges in gymnastics, swimming, and ice skating have more emotional than physical demands. Similarly, the umpire in tennis and volleyball and the scorer in softball are not required to perform physically strenuous duties.

"My doctor told me to get ready for the coming season by spending some time on the court."

In contrast, in boxing, wrestling, and water polo, the physical demands on officials increase. The referees in these sports literally follow the movement in the ring, on the mat, and at the sides of the pool. They are called upon to break clinches, get down on the mat to determine the legality of holds, and spot the ball.

In other sports, such as basketball, soccer, hockey, and football, the official must be as physically conditioned as the players. Thus an essential part of physical preparation for officials is a yearly preseason physical examination.

Physical Fitness

Officials need these physical fitness components to perform well: aerobic endurance and anaerobic capacity, strength, flexibility, speed, and coordination.[1] The importance of each component is determined by the nature of skills and the patterns of play involved in each specific sport.

However, no matter what sport you officiate, you will be better able to perform if you address the following fitness concerns:

- Cardiovascular endurance refers to conditioning the heart and circulatory system. Long, continuous aerobic movement is achieved from activities like walking, jogging, swimming, and cycling. Shorter bursts of movements with stops and starts depend on anaerobic conditioning. Running lines, jogging sprint distances, and performing change-of-direction activities develop this type of fitness.

- Strength is an important aspect of fitness. Sit-ups, pull-ups, and weight training under gradual overload regimens improve strength and build stamina.
- Flexibility increases the range of motion of joints, minimizes the probability of injury, and helps you relax by reducing muscle tension. You should stretch your muscles systematically to increase your range of motion, but don't force the stretch by bouncing.
- Diet and nutrition play an important role in physical preparation for performance. No exact rules exist concerning what and when you should eat. However, you should eat a variety of foods from the four basic food groups and determine the best time for you to eat before a contest.
- Rest or sleep is important for effective officiating. Although the amount of rest or sleep needed is highly individualized, the general rule of thumb is that people who are involved in rigorous training programs or participate in high-intensity sports require more rest than do sedentary individuals.

Pregame Warm-Up

In addition to achieving a healthy status in those five areas of fitness, you should always engage in some type of pregame warm-up. The dressing room is often an adequate area in which to limber up muscles and joints. Your warm-up routine helps your body tune up for the activities required of you in the upcoming contest. Be sure to include stretching, getting into particular body stances, doing calisthenics, running in place, and changing running directions. Remember, how you feel physically influences how you function mentally during a game.

PSYCHOLOGICAL PREPARATION

Your mental pregame routine plays a major role in your officiating performance. Mental preparation, concentration, and confidence are critical to good officiating. Your psychological routine should make you feel relaxed, alert, and in control throughout the contest. Include the following mental aspects of officiating in your routine to help you reach and maintain a high level of psychological functioning:

- Game strategy
- Flow
- Imagery
- Selective attention

Game Strategy

Too often referees or umpires arrive at the gym or field just before the contest. They haven't even thought about the game, much less devoted any time to pregame preparation, and their subsequent performance reflects their improvidence. That's why you should devise a game strategy before the start of the competition.

First, you must *analyze and list your strengths and weaknesses*. In what areas are you consistent? Where do you have trouble? Do your strengths complement those of the other officials? Are you tentative in your decision making? Can you sell the call? For pregame planning to work, you must be honest in your self-evaluation; otherwise, you'll continue to make the same mistakes.

Another aspect of developing a game strategy is to *learn about, in advance, the teams and the playing areas*. Veteran officials have an advantage over rookies in that they are familiar with the opposing teams, coaches, and playing environment. The experienced official has a mental advantage because he or she knows the playing styles of athletes and coaches, the typical size and behavior of the crowd, and the characteristics of the playing area (e.g., obstacles, surface, timing devices).[2] An inexperienced official must acquire such inside information by consulting with other officials, watching game tapes, and reading the local newspaper.

When developing your pregame plan, be alert to potential flaws in analyzing the situation. Never prejudge your assignment as an easy or tough one. This type of thinking leads to complacency or worry and focuses your attention on emotions rather than the demands of the contest.

Your strategic plan should also *deal with habitual mistakes*. For example, you may have a tendency to anticipate particular calls. Remind yourself that nothing can be called before it happens and that it is better to be a split-second late than to rule incorrectly. Good officials anticipate the play but not the call!

Going on the court or field without a carefully constructed plan of action is leaving yourself open for mistakes and subsequent criticism from players, coaches, and fans. Time devoted to game strategies before the event is a small sacrifice when you consider the benefits of improved officiating.

Flow

Officials must be more than good planners and technicians. They must also have a feel for the sport and how it is meant to be played. According to Jim Casada, coach and referee, some officials don't understand the "true nature" of the particular sport they are officiating.[3] They may be experts in the rules and officiating techniques, but lack that special appreciation for the sport's nuances.

It is not imperative for you to have played the sport you officiate, but if you haven't, you may have a hard time getting a real feel for the game. In an interview with five of the winningest high school football coaches, one of them made the point that "now, there are more officials who didn't play the game, and I think they're not as good as those who played."[4] Perhaps this perception results from the seemingly detached behavior of many officials. In contrast, an official who becomes totally immersed in his or her role during the contest will project the involvement players and coaches expect.

Experiencing Flow

You should watch as many games as you can, either in person or on television. Try to live the game with the players. Become familiar with specific skills executed by players; grasp a feeling for the ebb and flow of the game, and develop a sensitivity for the emotional overtones associated with the sport.

After you view the game from the players' perspective, put yourself back into the role of the official. Being able to see the game from different perspectives adds to your intuition of how the sport is meant to be played.

Your future as an official depends on your ability to combine both the science and the art of officiating. Years of experience are beneficial, but you can quickly gain the knowledge and intuition necessary to officiate effectively.

Imagery

Imagery helps you focus on the task at hand, both before and during the contest. Imagery is one of the most powerful mental techniques you can use in your pregame routine.

For example, imagine how you want to look and sound when you make a particular call. Play out certain situations in your mind. Visualize the penalties you might have to call. These actions will help you build confidence in your officiating skills and foster a positive attitude for the game.

Imagery involves mentally rehearsing correct officiating techniques. When you imagine your performance before the game, you are better able to concentrate on the task at hand and block out irrelevant thoughts during the game. Imagery occupies your mind with positive performance results and limits the amount of time you can spend on negative thoughts or feelings. Therefore, you are less likely to become nervous or psyched out.

You should use imagery during the week prior to the game. In addition, it should be the last thing you do before going out to the field, court, pool, gym, or track.

Selective Attention

Officials must attend to relevant cues and situations and block out meaningless ones. If you know which cues to pay attention to and which cues to ignore, you will be better able to concentrate on the key elements of the event.

Officials often err because of misdirected attention. For example, an inexperienced basketball official may focus on the ball at the expense of action away from the ball. Thus he or she will miss important aspects of the game such as a push-off for a rebound.

Knowing what to watch for is a critical ingredient for success, but an official must also be able to maintain that focus for a long period of time. Selective attention is not a temporary state. It refers to concentrating on relevant cues in your environment for the *duration* of the contest. Be aware that fatigue, interruptions in the flow of the game, and low motivation interfere with concentration and disrupt attentional focus.

Another attentional problem officials experience is adjusting their focus to meet the responsibilities of officiating a particular sport. Some sports require officials to have a narrow focus, such as the net umpire in tennis, the line judge in volleyball, or the finish line judge in track and field. In contrast, other officials need a broader focus, such as a basketball or football referee who must observe a wide field of activity.

Break!

Boxing referees need a Narrow-External Attentional Focus.

Concentration must be practiced, so make it part of your pregame routine. Your pregame routine to improve your selective attention should include the following:

• Reviewing officiating duties for the contest
• Developing a sequenced cue list (e.g., for a plate umpire the cue list might be infield, mound, ball, strike zone)

- Practicing blocking out irrelevant cues such as crowd noise or peripheral movements
- Watching game films and making calls while surrounded by loud sounds from a radio or people moving about the room

POSTGAME EVALUATION

Just as pregame rituals increase the probability of efficient performance, postgame routines can help you learn from the experience and improve your performance the next time out. Sport psychologists and motor behavior specialists advocate the use of feedback to improve skills.

Feedback refers to the information that officials obtain during and after a performance and can use to maintain or modify behaviors. What aspects of your officiating performance would you like to repeat in the same manner? In some of your techniques, were there flaws that require correction?

You can receive feedback visually, verbally, or kinesthetically (through your sense of movement). It can be self-obtained or provided by others. Research has indicated that feedback is more salient if (a) it is received shortly after the performance and (b) it includes qualitative (information about the execution of the skills) and quantitative (information about the outcome of the skills) factors.[5]

Based upon these findings, it is clear that officials should evaluate their performances relatively soon after the game. But the word *soon* doesn't mean that you have to rush home from a game and begin your evaluation immediately. In fact, you should take some time to relax and unwind after the contest, both physically and mentally.

The following day is a better time to reflect on your performance. If a videotape of the game is available, you can review your performance without relying on recall alone. Or you might seek out feedback from officiating peers or friends who watched the game. Timely and accurate feedback from these sources and your own reflections will direct and motivate you to perform well in future events.

The quantity of feedback refers to the *number* of times you "blew a call," "lost your cool," "stayed with the play," "made a hard but fair decision," and so forth. However, the quantity of feedback can be misleading because we more often remember spectacular rather than routine plays.

The quality of feedback reveals more about the *underlying reasons* for your performance. For example, high-quality feedback allows you to determine whether you missed a call because you were out of position or because you anticipated the play.

When you evaluate your own feedback, be honest in your appraisal. Use a checklist or chart to identify particularly strong or weak areas in your performance. When you receive feedback from others, be as receptive to the constructive criticism as to the compliments. In both situations, try to be systematic and objective in your analyses. Such a thorough postgame analysis should, in turn, help you to construct better pregame agendas.

SUMMARY

Officiating is physically and mentally demanding, before, during, and after the game. You must put a great deal of time and effort into pre- and postgame routines. Both physical and psychological preparation are necessary to officiate effectively. Postgame evaluation of feedback is particularly crucial to improving your performance in future contests.

Indeed, good officiating is a result of good pregame preparation and postgame evaluation. These routines will be easier for you to perform when you master the psychological skills of communication, confidence, motivation, relaxation, concentration, and imagery. In addition, each of these psychological skills will enable you to maximize your officiating performance.

PART II

Getting Along

Communication

3

Outstanding officials communicate effectively and understand that good communication skills are learned. They also recognize how crucial it is for officials to communicate effectively prior to the season with administrators; before games with associate officials and coaches; during games with players, coaches, and fans; and after games with other officials and the media.

The message you want to communicate is very specific. It conveys confidence, control, calmness, positive intensity, and fairness. It can be sent verbally or nonverbally. Your posture, your gestures and movements, and the tone of your voice combine to transmit either the right or the wrong message. As an official, your nonverbal messages will usually be more frequent and more powerful than your verbal messages.

Outstanding officials clearly and consistently send the right messages. So it is of great importance that you consider what message you're communicating as you perform and conscientiously work to improve your message-sending ability.

THE COMMUNICATION PROCESS

To communicate effectively you first need to understand the communication process, which consists of these six basic steps:

1. Deciding to send a message
2. Translating the thought to a concrete message
3. Sending the message
4. Getting the message through the proper channel
5. Receiving the message
6. Responding to the message

For example, you decide you would like to officiate for the 12-year-old soccer league in your community (Step 1). Then you must determine the key points you would like to get across to the league director, such as your willingness to give your time or an explanation of your background and experiences in soccer (Step 2). Next, you write a letter to the director and complete the official's application form (Step 3). Afterwards, you hand-deliver the letter and the application to the recreation department and ask that the forms be given to the director (Steps 4 and 5). The next afternoon, the director phones and invites you to attend an organizational meeting for all soccer officials on the following Tuesday (Step 6).

Sending the Message

Of the six steps of communication, the official should be most concerned with sending and receiving messages. Perhaps the most important decision you make as an official is when and how to send the message. Should you send the message upon entering the gymnasium for the volleyball match? Should the message be conveyed to coaches and captains prior to the game? Should the message be general or more specific in nature? Should the message be positive or negative? Will the player understand the message? These are but a few of the considerations involved in sending messages as an official.

Receiving the Message

Effectively receiving messages is also crucial for officials. Be mentally prepared to listen, and focus your attention on what the coach, player, or scorer is telling you. Listen with an open mind! You won't communicate effectively if you are evaluating or judging the message as it is being delivered. A common mistake is to stop listening to what the other person is saying and begin preparing your response. Avoid jumping ahead in this manner by paying attention to the entire message.

TYPES OF COMMUNICATION

Communication can occur *verbally* (by words) and *nonverbally* (by actions). Officials should be aware of these two types of communication, because *how* messages are sent is important.

Most of us believe that we communicate with others primarily through verbal means (reading, writing, speaking, and listening). Indeed, we do spend a good portion of each day communicating verbally. However, most communication between people is nonverbal, and the percentage of nonverbal communication for officials is even greater.

Although verbal and nonverbal skills are needed for effective communication, a greater percentage of messages is nonverbal in nature:

Body language   55%
Paralanguage   38% *how you say it*
Verbal language   7%

Note. From: "Communication Without Words" by A. Mehrabian, September 1968, *Psychology Today*, 52-55.

Nonverbal Communication

Nonverbal communication is typically organized into three categories:

- Body language (kinesics)
- Spatial relationships (proxemics)
- Paralanguage

Body Language

Body language is a powerful tool for an official. It includes your physical appearance, posture, touching behavior, gestures, and facial expressions.

Physical Appearance

We asked coaches, fans, and officials whether it was important for officials to look like athletes. Some said, "Officials owe it to the sport or teams to project an image of top physical and mental alertness," whereas others replied, "No, because we're officials and not athletes." The heart of the issue revolves around the nonverbal message that you relay in an official's uniform. You should exude a professional demeanor and a healthy, physically capable image. Such an appearance will project an image of control, credibility, and authority.

Posture

An erect posture signifies confidence, openness, and energy. In contrast, a slumped posture connotes feelings of inferiority and fatigue. Even the way you walk will communicate to others how you feel. A shuffling, slow walk with your head down reflects sad or unsure feelings, whereas a confident, energetic, rapid stride with your head up projects enthusiasm and self-assurance. The way you walk onto the field, into the gymnasium, or in an athletic facility will communicate your attitude toward the upcoming event. It also reflects your personality and professionalism.

Touching Behavior

Touching is a form of nonverbal communication that you can use to show respect, express affection, calm individuals, or gain attention. The handshake ritual between officials and coaches prior to a contest indicates mutual respect or appreciation of one another's contribution to the event.

However, in most sports, allowing any physical contact during a contest is taboo. You should maintain this practice to ensure respect for your decisions, to avoid undue friendliness between yourself and players, and to protect yourself from possible violent behavior directed toward you.

Gestures

Pointing a finger (reference to others), locking hands behind the back (openness), and rubbing the neck (anger or frustration) are examples of body language. The signals you employ when officiating to explain your rulings also are nonverbal forms of communication. For example, a football official raises both arms straight overhead to indicate a touchdown and a soccer official puts a hand on each hip to signal offsides.

Facial Expressions

The expression on a face sends a very direct message. A look that could "kill," a sneer, or a look of dismay leaves little doubt how a coach feels toward you or a call you've made. Similarly, an expression from you that communicates doubt or disinterest will be considered by the coach a clear signal of your inner thoughts about the contest.

In sum, your body language will be more effective if you walk with an erect posture that suggests you are alert and ready to officiate. Also, your appearance should be professional and consistent with the importance and type of event you're officiating. And remember, no matter what sport or level you are officiating, communicate composure and self-control.

Spatial Relationships

The way officials communicate is often dictated by the space between them and the participating athletes. Consider the case of a boxing referee in the ring. At times the referee must move in to observe all angles of the action. At other times, the official must step between the boxers to break a clinch or convey a message.

There are four zones or spaces in which we interact with others:[1]

- Intimate
- Personal
- Social
- Public

The zones differ according to the spatial distance between individuals. As an official, you will move in and out of all four of these spaces during the course of an event.

In some sports like basketball, softball, or wrestling, the space between officials and the players is at times close (intimate) and at other times comfortable (personal). Therefore, the potential for communication is increased. Frequently, a friendly discourse takes place between the first baseman and the first base umpire (personal), whereas nose-to-nose jawing occurs between the umpire and the manager over a controversial call (intimate). Similarly, basketball officials move up and down the court with the players, oftentimes exchanging instructional reminders or comments at a comfortable distance (personal). However, sometimes the referee moves into close (intimate) space to explain a call to the coach or to clarify some action or event to people at the scorer's table.

In contrast, the nature of certain athletic events favors a social zone. For example, tennis umpires and volleyball officials are somewhat removed from the playing area. They are placed in positions near the court where they render decisions in a businesslike manner. These standard distances between officials and tennis and volleyball players influence significantly the communication in these sports; a certain "distance" between athletes and officials is almost expected. That's why observers are so surprised when a tennis player gets into a close (intimate) confrontation with a line judge. Yet in baseball, such a player-umpire dispute is expected.

Paralanguage

Paralanguage refers to the vocal components of speech, separate from the actual meaning of the word. The adage "It's not what you say, but how you say it" explains what paralanguage is all about.

The pitch of your voice tends to get higher when you experience emotions such as joy, anger, or fear. Be aware of your feelings when you officiate and learn to control the pitch of your voice to fit the environment and particular situation.

Similarly, the tone of voice also sends a message. A loud voice conveys confidence, enthusiasm, and assertiveness, whereas a soft voice connotes understanding and trustworthiness. In some instances you will want to display an air of confidence about the call you made. In others, you will want a player or coach to know that you understand his or her message.

Because paralanguage is a powerful part of communication, ask yourself these questions:

• Does my voice have resonance (associated with firmness and strength)?

- Do I speak rapidly or slowly?
- Can I project in a loud voice?
- Can I control the pitch of my voice?

By answering these questions you will be able to identify personal weaknesses in the use of paralanguage. One helpful tool might be to tape one of your conversations and listen to your voice. You might be surprised at how it sounds. Use the tape to determine how to alter your voice to communicate more effectively as an official.

STYLES OF COMMUNICATION

Individuals tend to have a dominant communication style, but they also adopt alternate styles in specific situations. For example, even though you might favor give-and-take communication, your style of interaction will probably change when you meet with the supervisor of officials in your sport. This style of communication will differ dramatically from conversing with officiating colleagues. Indeed, communication styles are contingent on your relationship to the people involved in the exchange of information.

Four prominent communication styles and their characteristics are listed here:

- *Fighters*   Fighters are primarily concerned with achieving their own goals. They are interested in "winning" the discussion and have little interest in maintaining the relationship. They see relationships as a game, with a winner and a loser.

- *Negotiators*   Negotiators value their personal responsibilities and their relationships with others. They prefer a give-and-take approach. Officials who are negotiators listen to the frustrated coach or player and compromise when it is appropriate. They demonstrate authority but also show concern for the participant.

- *Dictators*   Dictators, like fighters, are primarily concerned with asserting their authority. They give directions and commands and revel in their power as officials. The dictator makes calls with the attitude, "I'm the boss," rather than the attitude, "I'm a vital part of this game." Often dictators place themselves above the contest and the participants.

- *Quitters*   Quitters give up and do nothing. They avoid confrontation and conflict with players, coaches, and spectators. They become intimidated when calls are openly questioned, and this leads them to withdraw and make fewer calls.

If you are concerned about the effectiveness of your communication, you first must recognize your predominant style. Then you have to determine whether that style is the most appropriate for your sport. The style of communication you emphasize will have a significant effect on your officiating performance, the relationships you establish, and the goals you are able to achieve.

COMMUNICATING WITH DIFFERENT GROUPS

The realities of sports place officials in an awkward position. You must maintain control over athletic contests and yet see to it that the game progresses with as little interference as possible on your part. In addition, you must communicate your decisions to fans, coaches, and players. Then, in turn, spectators, coaches, and participants send messages back to you—sometimes less than tactfully. Thus each contest you work requires you to interact with the variety of groups involved.

Players, Coaches, and Fans

An official who has a pleasant style, quick smile, and calm demeanor creates a positive environment that has a soothing effect on players and coaches. For example, a tennis umpire who uses the same tone to enforce a penalty point as he or she uses to announce the set score does not antagonize the penalized player and elicit an abusive reaction.

In contrast, a finger-pointing or verbal argument with a player or coach might demonstrate your certainty in the call but distorts the real message you want to communicate. Remember, communication is a two-way street. If you keep the lines of communication open, you will be more likely to have constructive and enjoyable relationships with athletes, coaches, and spectators.

A recent survey of high school basketball officials indicated that officials' style and nature of communication are influenced by interactions with players, coaches, and fans.[2] Approximately 41% of the officials surveyed said they were more demonstrative in making and signaling calls in front of hostile crowds; 30% said they made adjustments in hand signals and administration of the game depending upon the reaction of the crowd; and 36% admitted they were conscious of fan response when making unpopular calls.

An article in the magazine *Referee* suggests some keys to communicating with players, coaches, and spectators at any level:[3]

1. **Have your head on right**—Don't think your striped shirt grants you immunity from having to take a little criticism. It's part of officiating. Plan on it. Successful officials know how much to take. Ask one when you get the chance.

2. **Don't be a tough person**—If a coach is on your back but not enough so to warrant a penalty, then stay away from him or her. This is especially true during time-outs. Standing near an unhappy coach, just to "show him," will only lead to further tensions. Some officials develop irritating characteristics. Don't be one of them.

3. **Don't bark**—If you don't like to be shouted at, don't shout at someone else. Be firm with a normal relaxed voice. This technique will do wonders in helping you reduce the pressure. Shouting indicates a loss of control—not only of one's self, but also of the game.

4. **Show confidence**—Cockiness has absolutely no place in officiating. You want to *exude* confidence. Your presence should command respect from the participants. As in any walk of life,

appearance, manner, and voice determine how you are accepted. Try to present the proper image.

5. **Forget the fans**—As a group, fans usually exhibit highly emotional partisanship and delight in antagonizing the officials. Accepting this fact will help you ignore the fans, unless they interrupt the game or stand in the way of your doing your job.

6. **Answer reasonable questions**—Treat coaches and players in a courteous way. If they ask you a question reasonably, answer them in a polite way. If they get your ear by saying, ''Hey ref, I want to ask you something,'' and then start telling you off, interrupt and remind them of the reason for the discussion. Be firm, but relaxed.

7. **Choose your words wisely**—Don't obviously threaten a coach or player; this will only put them on the defensive. More importantly, you will have placed yourself on the spot. If you feel a situation is serious enough to warrant a threat, then it is serious enough to penalize, without invoking a threat. Obviously some things you say will be a form of threat, but using the proper words can make it subtle.

8. **Stay cool**—Your purpose is to establish a calm environment for the game. Nervous or edgy officials are easily spotted by

"Okay, it's just my word against yours -
but isn't that enough?"

fans, coaches, and players alike. Avidly chewing gum, pacing around, or displaying a wide range of emotions prior to or during a game will serve to make you seem vulnerable to the pressure.

Note. From: "Referee Checklist" by B. Mano, October, 1986, *Referee*, p. 58. Adapted by permission.

Associate Officials

One of the most satisfying experiences an official can have is to be a member of a team that gets along well and works together as a cohesive unit. A three-member crew in basketball or a seven-member team in football must function effectively as a unit if each individual is to accomplish her or his officiating objectives. Mutual respect, trust, acceptance, friendship, and encouragement are developed only if members of the officiating crews communicate with each other.

Steps for Effective Communication With Associates

Merely being together while traveling to and from games, at the contest site, or in social settings (e.g., officiating conferences, parties) does not necessarily increase good communication.

The key is establishing *open* communication. This type of interaction will allow you to prevent and solve problems *with* the help of your colleagues. Here are some suggestions for promoting openness among your associates:

- Get to know other members of the team.
- Avoid put-downs.
- Make an effort to get along with others.
- Encourage each other.
- Take responsibility for your own actions.
- Be honest when giving feedback to associates.
- Share your strengths and expertise.
- Seek advice or assistance from others.

Consistency Among Associates

Consistency is a key characteristic of effective officiating. The officiating within each crew needs to be consistent, but it takes teamwork to achieve it.

The degree of teamwork among officials varies from sport to sport. The rules of some sports dictate how much, when, and with whom officials communicate. In certain sports you are assigned specific duties and are expected to confine yourself to those responsibilities. For example, if you are calling lines in volleyball, you signal and call out in your area only. Officials with these responsibilities must limit themselves to these specified duties. However, if you are an independent judge in such sports as diving, gymnastics, or ice skating, you are a coactor with the other officials; and, your ratings should be somewhat consistent with those of the other judges. If your scores are always divergent from those of your colleagues, your abilities will be questioned by the performers, their coaches, the spectators, and the other judges.

In contrast, other sports allow more flexibility in assignments and greater interaction among the officiating team members. In football, each official begins the play with a specific set of duties. Once you have done your job, you can assist others as needed. Similarly, softball umpires have specific duties, but it is not uncommon for the plate umpire to ask for assistance from the first or third base umpire.

Optimal interaction among team officials is only possible if you and your colleagues

- demonstrate confidence in the ability of other officials by supporting their calls and actions and
- foster a team mind-set by cooperating when developing pregame, game, and postgame plans.

Communicating As a Unit

Effective communication between members of an officiating team or crew is not always easy to achieve. A crew that works together for an entire season has an advantage in that the officials are together for an extended time, they establish rapport, they complement each others' strengths and weaknesses in skill, and they learn how to communicate with each other. As NFL referee Jerry Markbriet said, "If you work hard at creating a close family tie with your crew, they'll perform better on the field because they're all good friends. There's no friction."[4]

Sometimes, however, personality conflicts develop between officials who work all their games together. Mendy Rudolph, a former NBA official, noted some of the pitfalls of a season-long pairing system: "If you do have bad habits, you never break yourself of them because you're working with the same guy all the time . . . and unless you really get along with each other you're going to have a lot of friction out there."[5]

Males and females are more and more frequently part of the same officiating team; a situation that poses additional problems for crew members' communication. Because men generally have had more involvement in sport, they sometimes feel superior to female associates (even when they are not) and attempt to dictate and control meetings and game situations. For example, if a male official tells a female colleague where to position herself or how to handle the game, the female will undoubtedly resent his instructions. This type of communication creates tension and places a strain on a contest that requires effective teamwork. The end result is that the quality of officiating suffers. Some female officials anticipate such negative attitudes by trying to show they're in control by using an authoritarian approach. But whether a male or female demonstrates this behavior, it will affect how the entire team of officials communicates with each other and with the players and coaches.

The nature of many sports at the professional, collegiate, high school, and recreational levels demands teamwork among officials, and teamwork demands good communication between each member of the officiating team. Personalities must mesh, officiating styles must be complementary, and partners must be sensitive to each other's needs. Your ultimate goal is to communicate with peer officials in a manner that facilitates the highest level of performance for the officiating unit.

POSTGAME COMMUNICATION

Effective communication must continue after the game. Officials can gain and share invaluable information and improve performance by communicating with other officials and the media.

Associate Officials

It should be clear by now that you can improve your performance by improving your communication skills. And one of the best ways for you to become a more practiced communicator, while at the same time building your confidence and maintaining your enthusiasm for officiating, is to openly discuss with colleagues your strengths and weaknesses following the contest. Ask colleagues who officiated the game with you for feedback. Be open to their compliments as well as their criticism, because you will need both types of comments to improve your officiating techniques for future contests.

You might also want to examine your own performance after the contest. Ask your own follow-up questions about the game, such as "Why did I make that call?" or "What are some of the areas I can improve in before the next contest?" Then evaluate how your responses compare to the feedback of colleagues.

Seek out advice from associates who are knowledgeable about officiating in your particular sport. They can help you analyze your performance and give you an honest appraisal of what you did well and what needs improvement.

Each of these postgame contacts can enhance your performance as an official. But if you don't communicate effectively, you'll miss out on the opportunity to improve your performance with the help of your colleagues. So make communication with associates a priority skill to develop.

Media

When games are hotly contested, or when the outcome of the game affects league standings, conference championships, or community pride, officials receive more than their share of media attention.

Such media coverage can influence your officiating in at least two major ways. First, concern over how your performance is being evaluated may produce undue anxiety and cause your confidence to wax and wane. And overanxiousness, overconfidence, and underconfidence lead to less than ideal game performances. Second, if you react emotionally to poor media coverage, it may build a barrier between you and reporters and limit positive communication.

Media Description of Officials

Because the media define and interpret sport for so many, they affect the way people perceive particular events. This is the case when fans

single out an official who has been cited for "missing" a call. A dozen replays, postgame analyses, and subsequent talk-show criticisms could seemingly alter even the official's spouse's viewpoint. The print media, too, are guilty of slanting fans' perceptions of officials. For example, during one week of the 1988 football season, local newspaper columnists blamed officials for the Dallas Cowboys' loss to the New York Giants ("Refs Don't Know the Rule") and the defeat of the University of North Texas by the University of Texas ("UNT 24, UT 20, Refs 7").

Coaches also add fuel to the fire. Some coaches, primarily those who lose, explain to the media the poor play of their teams or their losses by blaming an official. "They blew the call," "They were whistle-happy," or "They let the game get out of hand" are typical accusations. The media love such innuendos from coaches and will often keep prompting a coach to say something negative about the officiating, even when the coach has no gripe.

Furthermore, the media directly or indirectly portray officials as inconsistent and sometimes incompetent. An underlying complaint against officials is that they call fewer penalties against the home teams, the better skilled teams, and individuals who have been singled out as stars. In other words, according to some members of the media, officials enter games with a bias. Some officials are even stereotyped as individuals who carry grudges or use their power in the game to retaliate. Some announcers and reporters have suggested that umpires go out of their way to pick a fight (e.g., Dave Pallone and Pete Rose), that particular basketball squads get phantom calls, and that flags fly unfairly against certain football teams.

Officials' Perceptions of the Media

In contrast, a pet peeve of many officials is the lack of qualifications on the part of certain announcers and reporters. Officials insist that many of these individuals don't know the rules or fail to keep up with annual rule changes. They contend that media personnel should not be fans but objective reporters.

Your officiating has probably been scrutinized or chastised by the media. That's because the work you've chosen is public; your mistakes are public, and your competence is judged by the public. Thus, your mistakes will be difficult to hide. And the media certainly will do nothing to help you, the athletes, the coaches, or the fans forget your blunders. But they will also praise you for very good performances. The key to your communication with them is to acknowledge that the media will usually treat you fairly if you maintain a professional demeanor and attitude.

Tips for Communicating With the Media

The following suggestions won't alleviate your concerns about the media, but they will help you bridge the gap and eventually develop positive lines of communication:

- Don't talk with reporters and broadcasters if you haven't had a chance to collect your thoughts and get your emotions under control.
- Answer questions about rules or duties of officials but never comment on the play of teams or coaching abilities.
- Encourage your local board or league to appoint a spokesperson to reply to questions concerning officiating.
- Invite media personnel to attend your rules meetings and clinics.
- Treat the media with respect.

HOW TO IMPROVE COMMUNICATION

Before you can improve your communication skills, you must first understand exactly what you are currently saying and doing. To help you evaluate your communication skills, we've devised this Communication Skills self-test. Complete this test now and total your score.

Self-Help Test 3.1
Communication Skills Test

Directions: Respond to the following items by circling the number that corresponds to the description that most accurately reflects your behavior.

Rating Scale:	Never 1	Seldom 2	Usually 3	Always 4			
1. I like listening to others.				1	2	3	4
2. I state one thought at a time.				1	2	3	4
3. I pretend that I'm paying attention.				1	2	3	4
4. I use sarcasm.				1	2	3	4
5. I repeat key points.				1	2	3	4
6. I respect others' right to express themselves.				1	2	3	4
7. I am easily distracted by other noises.				1	2	3	4
8. I listen to all of the other person's message.				1	2	3	4
9. I finish thoughts for the speaker.				1	2	3	4

Rating Scale:	Never 1	Seldom 2	Usually 3	Always 4

10. I listen actively by nodding my head or verbally agreeing with what others are saying.   1 2 3 4

11. I keep the pitch of my voice level in tense situations.   1 2 3 4

12. I shake hands firmly.   1 2 3 4

13. I look directly at people when talking to them.   1 2 3 4

14. I walk slowly and hunch my shoulders.   1 2 3 4

15. I use my hands to augment my words.   1 2 3 4

Scoring the test: Simply add items 1, 2, 5, 6, 8, 10, 11, 12, 13, and 15 according to the actual numbers circled. Then, for items 3, 4, 7, 9, and 14, reverse the order of the numbering system. For example, if you circled "4" for the third item, you would score it as "1." Add these five reverse-scored items to the total for the first ten items summed to get your total Communication Score.

Rating Scale:	Total Score	Rating
	51 and up	Clear Connection
	40-50	Mixed Messages
	39 and below	Tongue-Tied

Once you have a handle on how you communicate, you may then decide to take steps to become a better sender or receiver of messages. Fortunately, several tools exist for improving the way you communicate as an official.

Logbook

Keeping a logbook makes you more aware of how you communicate. The act of writing something down serves to make it more real and concrete. That is why psychologists suggest that individuals who want to lose weight or stop smoking should keep a food and drink diary or a cigarette count, respectively. Such logbooks help identify undesirable patterns of behavior.

Use a communication logbook to record every aspect of your officiating performance. Record and evaluate your decisions and interactions after each contest. Use the following questions to help you evaluate your communication skills:

What one word best describes how I communicated?

Did I communicate best before, during, or after the event?

Which things did I communicate verbally and which nonverbally?

Did I communicate what I intended to?

Was my communication mostly positive or mostly negative?

Videotapes

If you want to improve your communication skills, you first need to know about your existing skills. A more direct method than self-questioning for gaining feedback about your communication is to review videotapes and record the frequency of your officiating communications. Specifically, count the number of instances in which you sent and received nonverbal messages through postures, touching behavior, gestures, and facial expressions. Then count the number of times there was actual verbal communication. Finally, if possible, distinguish between and count the volume levels and pitches of your voice. Examine the data from this videotape analysis and determine if there are weak areas that need to be addressed. The point of this exercise is to help you better understand the status of your communication skills. High scores on Self-Help Test 3.1 indicate that you receive and send verbal and nonverbal messages effectively.

Imagery

Imagery is a tool you can use to improve your communication (see chapter 8). However, the focus of your image must be on successful use of communication skills rather than on officiating performance.

For example, you might visualize a scene in which you are explaining a specific rule to a player. Visualize the proper spatial distance (personal) to use, the specific words that will best describe your interpretation of the rule, and the gestures that will enhance your presentation. Also include in your imagery what cues you will look for to indicate that the player understands your message. The main point is to visualize yourself communicating in a manner that benefits both of you.

SUMMARY

Communication consists of sending and receiving messages, both verbally and nonverbally. Officials primarily communicate nonverbally and therefore must learn how to more effectively send these types of messages. We have suggested that you seek out feedback and reflect on your style of communication to identify areas in which you are weak. You must also determine whether you are communicating effectively with others involved in the contest (athletes, coaches, spectators, and associate officials). Tools for enhancing your communication skills include logbooks, videotapes, and imagery.

Confidence

4

> For me, the most important thing is to be confident. Players and coaches can tell when officials are not confident in their calls. I try to be well prepared for my assignments, as that helps my confidence. Most officials know the rules and proper positioning. But you need to feel the confidence to carry out your role in a decisive, effective, and professional manner.

This quote from a college hockey official captures the critical role that confidence plays in being a competent and successful official. Confidence is one of the key characteristics of a good official (see chapter 1). Many officials we interviewed stated that having confidence is second only to knowing the rules and proper techniques of officiating in becoming an effective official. Research[1,2] in sport psychology indicates that confidence is the one factor that discriminates highly successful from less successful performers. Top sport performers, whether athletes or officials, consistently display a strong belief in *themselves* and their abilities.

DEFINING SELF-CONFIDENCE

When officials reflect on their performance, they often refer to how confident they felt. Comments such as "I really felt confident in my calls," "I felt confident that I could keep my composure," and "I just didn't act or feel confident out there" suggest the crucial role confidence plays in officials' own self-evaluations of performance.

Although the word *confidence* is used frequently, few people can define exactly what it really is. Sport psychologists define confidence as *the belief that you can successfully perform a desired behavior.* That behavior might be making a critical call at the end of a game, controlling an unruly crowd, or positioning yourself to make a call. The most significant aspect of self-confidence, however, is believing in your ability to do the job. A high school basketball official alludes to this critical element of confidence:

> The key thing is that you always try to be positive. As an official you are always wrong 50% of the time according to the players or coaches. Everyone is going to miss some calls but you can't let that get you down. I always try to make my calls in a confident, self-assured manner and convey to the players that I am in control. I always try to do my homework and prepare for the game, as that builds my own sense of confidence. If I feel confident in myself and my abilities, then everything else seems to fall into place.

Confident officials believe in themselves and their ability to meet the challenges and decisions they face during an athletic contest. Officials who lack confidence doubt whether they are good enough or have what it takes to make the tough calls and keep things under control at all times. Such self-doubt puts psychological barriers on these officials because expectations can have a profound impact on one's performance and success.

OVERCOMING PSYCHOLOGICAL BARRIERS

We defined self-confidence as the belief that you can successfully execute a desired behavior. When you expect to succeed and believe in your ability to officiate competently, you are creating a self-fulfilling prophesy. This means that expecting something to happen actually helps cause it to happen.

Unfortunately, some officials doubt their ability to succeed or to acquire the skills necessary to be good officials, and the result is a negative self-fulfilling prophesy. Negative self-fulfilling prophecies generate a vicious cycle in which expectation of failure leads to actual failure, which further lowers self-image and, in turn, increases expectations of future failure.

A Case Study

A classic example of how psychological barriers influence performance occurred in track and field. The specific case involved breaking the 4-minute barrier in the mile run. A number of runners were timed at 4:03, 4:02, and 4:01, but nobody could crack the 4-minute barrier. Some observers even went so far as to claim that a "sub-4" mile was physiologically impossible. Most runners agreed.

Roger Bannister, however, did not. He was sure that he could break the 4-minute barrier under the right conditions, and he did. Although this was an impressive athletic feat, in the next year more than a dozen runners broke the 4-minute mile.

Why should this occur? Did everyone all of a sudden get faster or start training harder? Of course not. The runners finally believed that it actually could be done! Until Roger Bannister broke the barrier, however, runners were limited by their belief that it was impossible to break the 4-minute mile.

The 4-minute mile example applies to your own officiating situation. You too must be aware of and prepared to break down psychological barriers. It's easy to get down on yourself after you miss a call or two. However, it's extremely important to continue to have confidence in your officiating capabilities. Maintaining confidence under adversity is the key, as noted by this male professional tennis umpire:

> The chair umpire in tennis is a job that requires individuals who have confidence in themselves and are not easily shaken. The players hit the ball so hard and fast and close to the lines that it is virtually impossible to be absolutely certain of all the calls. And even if you are doing a good job, usually one of the players or the spectators think you are blind. But the important thing is that you can't start to doubt yourself, because once you do you start to lose control of the match. In the end the players will also respect you and your calls more if you show them that you are confident in your judgment and your abilities.

CHARACTERISTICS OF CONFIDENT OFFICIATING

Confidence is characterized by a high expectancy of success. It involves believing that you have the capacity to perform the actions required for success—that there is a high probability that you will exhibit these behaviors, and that there is a high probability that success will result from these actions. In short, confidence will help you be a better official by enhancing your ability in the following areas:

- Concentration
- Control
- Goal setting
- Persistence

Concentration

Confidence facilitates focused concentration on the task at hand. When you are feeling confident your mind is free to remain focused on the job of officiating: Nothing else intrudes.

When you lack confidence, you tend to worry about how well you are doing or how well others think you are doing rather than staying focused on the game. A preoccupation with avoiding failure that results from a lack of confidence will impair your concentration by making you more easily distracted.

Control

When you are confident you are more likely to be relaxed and feel in control, especially in adverse situations. This is critically important for an official because you will inevitably have to make difficult calls and deal with unhappy or irate players, coaches, and fans. Self-confidence enables you to feel in control and project a sense of self-assurance. This appearance alone sometimes prevents arguments and intimidating behavior from erupting.

Goal Setting

Confident individuals tend to set challenging goals and actively pursue those goals. Officials who are not confident, however, tend to set easy goals and thus never really push themselves to be the best that they can be. We provide a thorough discussion of goal setting in chapter 5.

Persistence

Research in sport psychology has consistently found that confidence is a major determinant in both the amount of effort an individual puts forth to achieve a goal and how long he or she will persist in pursuit of the goal.[3,4] Good officials are committed and have a desire to excel in their role. Confidence in your abilities will help you hang in there even when you don't seem to be making as much progress as you would like.

CONFIDENCE AND PERFORMANCE

In chapter 1 we listed confidence as one of the most important characteristics of a competent official, and, as such, it is a critical factor in determining your effectiveness and the outcome of your performance. However, we have not really addressed the specific relationship between confidence and performance. First of all, confidence won't overcome incompetence. You simply must know the rules of your sport and the mechanics of officiating it. Without those skills, confidence can take you only so far.

The relationship between confidence and performance is similar to the relationship between anxiety and performance (see chapter 6). That

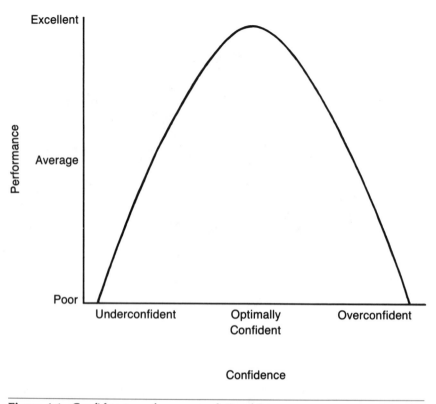

Figure 4.1 Confidence-performance relationship.

is, there is an inverted-U relationship between confidence and performance (see Figure 4.1). Performance improves as your level of confidence increases up to an optimal point, whereupon further increases in confidence produce corresponding decrements in performance.

Optimal self-confidence means being totally convinced that you can achieve your goals and that you will strive hard to do so. Self-confident officials acknowledge their limits and have realistic expectations. Having self-confidence does not necessarily guarantee that you will always perform well, but it is essential to reaching your potential as an official. You are still going to blow some calls, be out of position, and lose your cool at times, but believing in yourself will help you deal more effectively with these problems and keep you striving to be the best.

Each person has an optimal level of self-confidence, and problems arise when an official has either too little or too much confidence. We now take a closer look at how being either overconfident or underconfident will affect your officiating performance.

Lack of Confidence

We have discussed how individuals place psychological limits on themselves when they lack confidence in their abilities. Indeed, many officials we interviewed said that self-doubt had been a problem at one time or another in their careers. Although they had confidence in their technical skills and knowledge of the game and rules, some officials still were unsure of their ability to officiate. Their diffidence (lack of confidence) was especially apparent regarding championship games and the presence of a hostile crowd.

Such self-doubts undermine officiating performance by creating anxiety, breaking concentration, and causing indecisiveness. Officials lacking confidence frequently focus on their shortcomings rather than on their strengths, thus distracting them from concentrating on their work. A baseball umpire we interviewed described how a lack of confidence limited his effectiveness early in his career:

> When I first started umpiring, I just didn't have confidence in my calls and judgment. I wouldn't be decisive and my calls would lack conviction. I was always afraid of blowing a call and wanted to be liked by players and fans alike. However, as I got my experience I started to feel more comfortable and confident in myself as a person, and I think this was evident in my play calling. I knew that I had prepared myself well and that my main goal was to call a fair game. My calls became clear, strong, and decisive; and it was my confidence that eventually won the respect of the players and coaches.

Overconfidence

Individuals who are overconfident are actually falsely confident, that is, their confidence is actually greater than their real abilities warrant. And their performance declines because they believe that they don't have to prepare themselves or put forth the effort required to get the job done. As a general rule, this is not as problematic as underconfidence, but when it occurs the effects can be just as disastrous.

An official's overconfidence is reflected by a lack of preparation for games. Thinking that you are better than you really are and that you don't need to prepare is a sure course to failure. Underestimating the need to prepare for each game and not taking the time to be aware of the specific rules that govern each competition are signs of overconfidence.

Confidence is based on preparation, hard work, and the development of the competencies necessary to be an effective official. If you take these things for granted, you are taking the first step toward over-confidence, which will ultimately cause you to perform below your capabilities.

ASSESSING YOUR CONFIDENCE

Now that you know about the optimal level of confidence, you should try to identify how confident you feel in a variety of officiating situations. The following questions should help you do this:

When am I overconfident?

How do I react to adversity?

Am I afraid of certain situations?

How do I recover after making a bad call?

Is my confidence consistent throughout the competition?

Do I look forward to and enjoy a tough assignment?

Am I tentative and indecisive in certain situations?

Use your responses to these questions as a starting point for getting in touch with your feelings of confidence. They may help you identify the situations in which your confidence is high or low. For a more formal and detailed assessment of your officiating confidence, complete the Officiating Confidence Inventory in Self-Help Test 4.1.

Self-Help Test 4.1
Officiating Confidence Inventory

This inventory will help you evaluate your confidence about various characteristics of yourself that are important to being a successful official. As you know, we can have too little confidence, too much confidence, or just the right amount of confidence. Read each question carefully and think about your confidence with regard to each item. Respond in relation to how you have felt while officiating over the past year. For each item indicate the percent of time you feel you have had too little, too much, or just the right degree of confidence. First comes an example of how to fill out the inventory correctly.

	Under-confident	Confident	Over-confident	
How confident are you that you can control an irate player?	30%	60%	10%	= 100%

The total percent for all three answers should always be 100%. You may distribute this 100% any way you think is appropriate. You may assign all 100% to one category, split it between two categories, or as in the example, divide it among all three categories. Remember, you are to indicate the percent of time when you officiate that you feel you have too little, just about the right amount of, or too much confidence.

	Under-confident	Confident	Over-confident
With respect to your ability to . . .			
Keep calm under pressure	_____ %	_____ %	_____ %
Maintain self-control	_____ %	_____ %	_____ %
Relate successfully to other officials	_____ %	_____ %	_____ %
Communicate with coaches and athletes	_____ %	_____ %	_____ %
Concentrate throughout a game	_____ %	_____ %	_____ %
Make tough calls decisively	_____ %	_____ %	_____ %
Make critical decisions	_____ %	_____ %	_____ %
Put forth the effort to succeed	_____ %	_____ %	_____ %
Persist to achieve your goal	_____ %	_____ %	_____ %
Improve your technique	_____ %	_____ %	_____ %
Control your emotions	_____ %	_____ %	_____ %

(Cont.)

Self-Help Test 4.1 (Continued)

	Under-confident	Confident	Over-confident
Handle an irate coach or player	_____ %	_____ %	_____ %
Be assertive in making calls	_____ %	_____ %	_____ %
Maintain a high level of physical fitness	_____ %	_____ %	_____ %
Be mentally prepared for your assignments	_____ %	_____ %	_____ %
Deal effectively with an unruly crowd	_____ %	_____ %	_____ %

To score your overall confidence, add up the percentages in each of the three columns and then divide by 16. The higher your score on the "Confident" column, the more likely you are to be at your optimal level of confidence while officiating a competition. High scores on the "Under-confident" or "Over-confident" columns present some potential problem areas. If you want to focus on your specific strengths and weaknesses, just look at the specific items that refer to the different aspects of officiating. You should note that the scale assesses confidence for both your physical and your mental skills.

Use the information gained from this questionnaire to address some of the areas where your confidence is not as high as you would like it to be.

BUILDING YOUR CONFIDENCE

A common misconception in sport is that a performer can do little to build confidence. Many people simply believe that either you have it or you don't. We view confidence as a psychological skill that can be learned.

The remainder of the chapter presents strategies and techniques for improving your confidence. Specifically, you can improve your confidence through the following:

- Thoughts (self-talk)
- Actions
- Imagery

- Performance accomplishments
- Physical conditioning
- Preparation

Think Confidently

Confidence consists of thinking that you can and will do what you set out to do and that you will have success doing it. You need to practice thinking confidently because this makes your self-talk more positive.

Positive self-statements make you more confident when you officiate. In short, if you *think* you will make the correct calls and keep control of the game, then you probably will. That's why it is so important to eliminate all the negative things you say to yourself and keep yourself thinking positively and confidently.

For example, you need to discard such negative thoughts as "I'll never be a good official," "What a stupid call," or "I just can't keep control of the game," and replace them with positive thoughts such as, "I'll keep getting better if I work at it," "That'll be the last call I'll blow this game," or "I am going to bring the players together and make it clear that I will enforce the rules."

Your thoughts should be positive and motivational rather than judgmental. That's not always easy for an official to do, given the negative feedback usually dished out by spectators, athletes, and coaches. But work at it, and you'll have a more enjoyable and successful officiating experience. Self-talk is discussed in more detail in chapter 6.

Act Confidently

Because your thoughts, feelings, and behaviors are interrelated, the more you act confidently, the more likely you will be to feel confident. Don't doubt yourself or your abilities—athletes and coaches will immediately pick up on your insecurity and try to take advantage of you. Instead, project an appearance of confidence, and your doubt will disappear.

You demonstrate your confidence by making decisive calls, even when you are not sure whether you made the correct decision. For example, balls in volleyball and tennis that hit near an out-of-bounds line should be called instantly and with conviction, even if you are less than certain of where the ball hit the court. Such decisive action reflects certainty and conveys a sense of control.

Another way officials can act confidently is through the use of the voice. A resonant, strong voice is a great asset to an official in those sports where decisions are communicated verbally, such as basketball, baseball, and tennis. With a clear, strong voice you convey

confidence in your decisions. A firm, properly pitched voice will help you feel more poised and confident to make subsequent calls.

Image Success

One of the important uses of imagery is helping to build confidence. Imagery allows you to see yourself doing everything correctly, even though you might actually have trouble performing some of your officiating tasks.

Imagery will also help you prepare for an upcoming assignment. For example, you might go over situations in your mind that have caused you difficulty in the past and imagine yourself dealing with them successfully. If you know you have trouble working with a certain official, you might visualize yourself communicating effectively with this person in situations that have caused problems in the past. Or, if you know that players in an upcoming game are likely to be overly rough and aggressive, you can visualize yourself being strong, poised, and assertive in establishing control right from the start of the game. So boost your confidence and prepare yourself for upcoming officiating assignments by visualizing yourself dealing effectively with any problems that might arise. A more detailed description of imagery is presented in chapter 8.

Get Experience

Research has indicated that the most powerful builder of confidence is performance accomplishments.[5,6] The concept is simple: Having performed a behavior successfully in the past will increase your confidence that you can perform it successfully in the future. In the case of an official, confidence is gained through experiences such as officiating a championship game, controlling a large angry crowd, making crucial calls at the end of a game, coping effectively with player and coach outbursts, and working together with other officials.

Of course, this is not always as easy as it sounds. For example, National Football League referee Pat Haggerty was singled out by the press for blowing two calls in the first few games of the 1988 season. Specifically, he mistakenly called a safety against the Dallas Cowboys in their 12-10 loss to the New York Giants. Then, Haggerty was accused of unjustly calling a roughing-the-passer penalty against the Kansas City Chiefs that nullified an interception and allowed the San Diego Chargers to score the winning touchdown two plays later. After these two situations, Pat Haggerty could have lost confidence in his decision-making abilities. Instead, he drew upon his vast experience and reflected on all the good calls that he has made throughout the years.

You might wonder how can you be confident without previous successes. Specifically, do you need to be confident to perform effectively as an official or do you need to be a competent official before you become confident? The answer to both questions is "No, but it helps." Or, as a soccer official told us: "I'm doing a much better job now because I have gained confidence; the reason I'm confident is that I've been doing real well."

There are several steps you can take to build confidence:

1. Practice your skills and techniques to build confidence for actual game situations.
2. Seek out officiating opportunities in relatively low-key situations. For example, many organized youth sport leagues need officials but do not involve high-pressure situations because they focus more on learning skills than on winning. These are especially good situations in which to gain valuable experience, practice skills and techniques, and thus enhance confidence.

3. Attend officiating clinics and workshops that offer an opportunity to learn new techniques and provide additional practice. These settings are particularly valuable for practicing and perfecting techniques and for receiving feedback from peers regarding your performance.

4. Get as much actual experience as you can to build your confidence and make you a better official.

Get Fit

In sports such as basketball and soccer the quality of officiating is strongly affected by the physical condition of the official. Physical fitness is necessary for officials in these sports to maintain proper positioning, be alert, exercise good judgment, and encourage teamwork.

Even if you officiate a sport that does not require much activity, such as tennis or baseball, it is important to be in good physical condition. If you aren't, fatigue will set in, judgment will become less accurate, and overall performance will decline throughout the event.

Perhaps you are scoffing at the importance we're placing on physical fitness. Then answer this: Why do world class chess masters spend so much time working out? These players know that, even though chess is a cerebral game, they have to be in good physical condition to maintain concentration for long periods of time. Because one bad decision or lapse in concentration can spell disaster in a chess match, chess masters maintain that being in good shape enhances their ability to stay alert over the course of what can be a grueling mental challenge. Their fitness, therefore, makes them confident that they can still be at the top of their game no matter how long the chess match takes.

The same is true for a chair umpire in tennis. Suppose the umpire has officiated a 3-hour match that has gone to a tiebreaker in the last set. If the umpire is fatigued and thus distracted by his or her own physical state, that official's ability to concentrate will be severely hindered.

Finally, in talking to coaches, athletes, and spectators, we discovered another apparent reason for officials to be in good condition. Put simply, participants and observers have more respect for, and confidence in, officials who take good care of themselves. So if you want to be at your best and receive the respect of participants and fans, get in shape and stay in shape! Your fitness can also serve as a source of confidence because you'll feel better prepared to meet the mental and physical challenges of officiating a long and grueling competitive event.

Preparation

As discussed in chapter 2, you must prepare for each assignment to be in top form. So do your homework until you feel capable of handling any situation that might arise. This might involve going out to the site of the contest beforehand and examining its layout and condition. You might also review the coaches and athletes in the contest to see if there is anything you need to be particularly ready for based on their reputations or your own experience. Such mental preparation for an event also increases your confidence. This confident attitude, in turn, helps you establish and maintain control of the competition.

SUMMARY

Confidence involves the way you feel, think, and act. Because these are so closely tied together, it is important that you strive to gain and maintain confidence in each of these areas. This chapter has demonstrated the critical role that confidence plays in your officiating. You must believe in your mental and physical abilities to be a competent official. Strive for a strong sense of confidence without becoming overconfident or underconfident. Your level of confidence will almost certainly fluctuate at times, but you always need to believe in yourself and your capabilities. Officials who lack confidence in themselves are going to experience a rough road, so take the paths that systematically build your confidence by using the suggestions provided in this chapter.

PART III

Getting Psyched

Motivation

5

"You've got to love the game, really love it. You must enjoy the game as you work it."

We have discussed several different ways in which psychological skills can greatly enhance your effectiveness at officiating. And developing a psychological skills training program to cope with anxiety, improve concentration, and utilize imagery will certainly help you approach and carry out your job as an official. But, without the proper motivation, desire, and commitment, you are not likely to follow through on such a program.

Although most officials start off with a lot of desire and motivation, they find it difficult to maintain that high level of motivation game in and game out over the course of their careers. As one major league umpire stated, "I think every umpire who works in the minor leagues thinks once or twice about quitting." Officials typically receive little in the way of financial rewards, and it is unusual to receive praise and positive reinforcement from players, coaches, fans, or the media. Despite this fact, you still have to work to the best of your ability every time you take the floor, field, or court. You also need to be aware of the potential for burnout, which we discuss in-depth in chapter 9.

Consequently, you need a strong sense of self and a high level of motivation to overcome the lack of praise and ample criticism you'll receive as an official. You can't be overly concerned about how other people view or evaluate your performance. Rather, you must focus on self-perceptions of performance and progress. As long as you see yourself improving and advancing toward meaningful goals, then the chances are extremely high that you will maintain a high level of motivation.

Indeed, goal setting plays a critical role in your motivation and commitment to officiate. Goals provide a sense of direction and a challenge for the future. As Keith Bell[1] aptly notes in his book *Championship Thinking*, "Floundering in the world of sport without setting goals is like shooting without aiming. You might enjoy the blast and kick of the gun but you probably won't get the bird."

Although people are generally aware of what goals are and why they are important, few understand the principles that make goals work. In this chapter we acquaint you with the principles of goal setting. We obtained most of the information from goal setting research conducted in organizational settings, and more recent studies of athletes. However, officials are similar to athletes in that they are constantly trying to improve their sport performance. Thus, it makes sense that the principles of goal setting that have been successful for a variety of laborers and athletes would also hold true for officials.

We begin by defining *goal* and identifying why goals work. Then we present the guidelines for setting up a goal-setting program that you can use in officiating. Finally, we offer additional ways to help maintain your motivation for officiating over the course of several seasons.

DEFINITION OF GOALS

A goal is the *aim or purpose of an action*. Put simply, goal setting is a means of identifying what you want to accomplish and when you plan on accomplishing it. Edwin Locke, one of the top researchers in the area of goal setting, defines a goal as attaining a specific standard of proficiency on a task, usually within a specific time limit.[2] Regardless of the precise definition, a goal usually focuses on achieving some standard of excellence, whether it be to get in better position to make close calls, to be more decisive in making your call, or to keep calm under pressure.

WHY GOALS WORK

More and more people in business education and sport are using goals to help improve productivity and performance. The beneficial effect of goal setting on performance is one of the most consistent and strongest findings in the psychological literature. In fact, in 99 out of 110 studies reviewed by Locke and his colleagues, people who set specific hard goals exhibited significantly higher levels of performance than individuals who set easy goals, no goals, or do-your-best goals.[3] So, let's examine why goals have such a significant impact on improving performance.

Goals Help Determine What's Important

Many people become involved in officiating because they simply enjoy sports and competition. Officiating is one way for them to stay close to that environment. But this initial impetus will probably be insufficient to maintain your interest for a long period of time. Goals can help you determine exactly what you want to get out of officiating.

You will need to set some specific goals to define what you want to accomplish. These goals should be related to why you became an official in the first place. In other words, your goals should serve as stepping stones leading to your ultimate destiny as an official. Just make sure that the stones (goals) aren't too far apart (i.e., they don't increase dramatically in difficulty) or you'll likely fall short and become discouraged.

Goals Increase Effort and Direct Attention

If you set an important goal for yourself, you will generally put forth more effort to achieve that goal. Specifically, if your goal is to make sure that you are in good position to make tough calls, then you will typically try harder to reach that goal.

A basketball official, for example, might work very hard to stay fit because then he'll be able to get up and down the court easier and be in a better position to make the calls. And because the official's goal is to get in good shape, his future behavior is more likely to include activities that accomplish that objective. Thus the official will focus on diet and exercise.

Another official might want to improve her officiating technique and knowledge of the game. And, therefore, the official attends a number of officiating camps and seeks out information in books and other sources to acquire the knowledge she desires.

From these two examples, you can see that goals can help you improve as an official, both physically and mentally.

Goals Help Maintain Motivation

Regardless of what profession or activity you are pursuing, you must be motivated to live up to your potential. Officials are seldom rewarded by a constant stream of accolades. Rather, the only time that most officials receive attention is when they are perceived to have blown a call, lost control of the crowd, or gotten into a big altercation with a coach or an athlete. Thus officials in particular find it hard to maintain motivation.

Although you are certainly motivated from time to time (as you are now in reading this book), goals will help you stay motivated over a long period of time. Setting goals for personal improvement rather than praise or recognition from others will allow you to experience self-satisfaction, independent of other sources. Continually striving to meet self-set goals is a consistent and powerful source of motivation.

GOAL-SETTING GUIDELINES

It would be misleading to suggest that setting any type of goal will improve your performance or that all goals will be equally effective. In fact, certain kinds of goals work better than others. Sport psychologists have developed goal-setting guidelines that maximize performance and motivation. These guidelines direct you to do the following:

- Identify your goals
- Set challenging but realistic goals
- Make your goals positive
- Set short- and long-term goals
- Write down your goals
- Identify strategies to reach your goals

Identify Your Goals

When first getting started, you must first determine exactly what it is that you want to achieve. One way to identify your goals is to ask yourself a series of questions about your skills and attitudes toward officiating.

What are my greatest strengths as an official?

What are my greatest weaknesses as an official?

What aspects of officiating are most enjoyable to me?

Do I prepare myself mentally for each game?

Am I in good physical condition?

Do I communicate well with other officials, players, and coaches?

Am I well versed in the rules and regulations?

Are my mechanics and positioning sound?

As you address these questions, you will realize that the answers are not necessarily straightforward or simple. But just thinking about these things should help clarify what you want to accomplish through your officiating and identify specific areas for improvement.

Set Challenging But Realistic Goals

It has been demonstrated that the more difficult the goal, the better the performance, as long as the person is capable of achieving the goal. But don't try to be a perfectionist and set goals that are unrealistic or impossible. Being an official is a difficult job, and it is unrealistic to expect that you will officiate a perfect game, just as it is unrealistic for a basketball player to expect to make all of his or her shots on a given night.

Similarly, you should not set goals that are too easy because such goals will severely limit what you achieve. If you set your goals too low you might be satisfied with performance that is less than your best. For example, if your goal is simply to be chosen for a particular assignment, then you might be satisfied just to be there instead of focusing on doing a good job.

Make Your Goals Positive

Always word your goals positively. That is, try to identify the things you would like to do instead of the things you don't want to do. Telling yourself not to do something calls attention to the undesired act. If there is a behavior you want to reduce in frequency or to eliminate, set a goal to do an alternative, positive behavior.

For example, if you want to reduce the number of times you hesitate too long before making a call, don't set a goal not to hesitate. Rather, set a goal to improve your decisiveness by practicing making calls immediately after you blow your whistle. In addition, use imagery to reinforce your positive goal. Imagine yourself in situations where you have been indecisive in the past and visualize yourself blowing your whistle and making a quick, decisive call in an assertive, confident manner (you will learn more about imagery in chapter 8). This will help you focus on responding successfully in a situation that has been troublesome, a response you want to become almost automatic.

Set Short- and Long-Term Goals

When you ask people what their goals are, they invariably mention very ambitious long-term goals such as being president of the company, becoming a millionaire, or going to medical school. Officials also tend to set their sights on such grand goals, like making it to the professional ranks.

Although long-term goals are important, research shows that short-term goals are *essential* for two reasons.[4]

One reason is that short-term goals provide feedback on how you are progressing toward your long-term goal. For example, if your long-term goal is to be a professional sport referee, you can monitor your progress toward that goal every time you officiate with short-term goals. Your short-term goals might include improving your knowledge of the rules, being more decisive, staying calm under pressure, communicating better with athletes and coaches, or becoming more confident. The key is that short-term goals provide a standard to shoot for in each officiating performance, and they provide feedback concerning your progress toward your long-term goal.

⋇The second reason short-term goals are critical is that they are a vital source of motivation. It is sometimes hard to look down the road and actually believe that you will accomplish your long-term goal because it seems so far away. It is much easier to maintain motivation if you can see improvement in your performance every time you officiate a game. That does not mean that you will improve with every game, but short-term goals provide a yardstick by which to evaluate progress each time you put on your officiating uniform.

Write Down Your Goals

People who fail to write down their goals often fail to attain them. Writing down your goals will increase your commitment to them. Goals are useless unless you are committed to them. Having a record of your goals and the progress you are making toward them is one good way to ensure commitment, effort, and persistence. In other words, charting your own improvement on paper helps you to hang in there during the difficult times.

A good way to keep an accurate account of your goals is to start a notebook that contains your written goal statements and achievements. Such a recording system provides written feedback that can serve as a powerful motivator and sustain your efforts over time. You can keep chronological records for charting your progress over time. These records will help you monitor improvement and allow you to adjust your goals should you find them too easy or unattainable.

Identify Strategies to Reach Your Goals

Although goals provide direction, you still must map out a strategy to get there. For example, suppose one of your goals is to improve your conditioning so that you can sustain a high level of performance throughout each officiating assignment. What are you going to do to improve your conditioning? At this point, you need to identify a strategy to help you reach your goal. In this case it might involve exercising at least four times a week for 30 minutes each session or reducing your caloric intake by 500 calories a day. The important point is that you identify what you will do to achieve your goals.

ADDITIONAL MOTIVATIONAL STRATEGIES

Although goal setting is perhaps the most effective means for enhancing motivation, other approaches exist for staying motivated and involved in officiating. Let's take a quick look at these alternative approaches. We hope some of them will work for you.

- Find inspiration in models
- Reward yourself for a job well done
- Develop a social support network
- Nurture intrinsic motivation

Find Inspiration in Models

No matter what the field of endeavor, we all can find inspiration in watching the performances of highly successful performers. Athletes such as Michael Jordan, Carl Lewis, Wayne Gretzky, Steffi Graf, Jerry Rice, Jackie Joyner-Kersee, or Don Mattingly inspire future sport stars when they perform their specialty.

Great officials can serve the same function. You, as an aspiring or practicing official, can learn a great deal from such expert officials as Jim Tunney (football), David Socha (soccer), Earl Strom (basketball), and Marty Springstead (baseball). You can also look to the many, many excellent officials working at amateur levels of competition as models and sources of information. You can learn a lot from these successful officials. Rely on them as a source of motivation and inspiration throughout your career.

Reward Yourself for a Job Well Done

Officials often must reward themselves for doing a good job because rarely will they receive recognition or praise from players, coaches, spectators, or the media. One of the most powerful reinforcers you can give yourself is self-rewarding thoughts, or self-talk.

For instance, after a game in which you felt that you did a particularly good job, tell yourself, "Way to go," "That's the way to keep things under control," "I really kept my cool," or "I'm getting a lot better each game." This rewarding self-talk is often accompanied by a warm, good feeling of accomplishment for doing a competent, professional job. This type of self-reward not only feels good but also helps us maintain our motivation and commitment.

Besides rewarding yourself through self-statements, you might also use material rewards. You're not likely to get any extra money from the league office if you happen to officiate a really great game. How-

"It was just too much for him . . .
the losing coach told him he did a good job."

ever, that does not mean that you can't reward yourself for a really excellent performance. Going out to a movie, buying yourself some clothes, eating out at your favorite restaurant, or getting tickets to a special sporting event are just a few ways you can reward yourself. These little rewards provide tangible acknowledgement of a job well done and make officiating more fun and satisfying.

Develop a Social Support Network

It is important to develop your own group of acquaintances that you can turn to when necessary. You might want to get together periodically with other officials who share some of your same frustrations and experiences and who can appreciate your difficult task. Officiating cohorts also provide good feedback concerning your performance as an official. You will probably find out that the things that trouble you also trouble other officials. In addition, from the experience of other officials you might pick up some good pointers that you can incorporate into your own style.

Another good way to develop social support is through attendance at officiating conferences and workshops. Such settings will allow you to stay on top of the latest developments in the profession and interact with your peers. By staying abreast of the latest developments and rule changes, you'll feel more motivated to perform well in future assignments. Social support networks are addressed more extensively in chapter 9.

Nurture Intrinsic Motivation

In a recent survey that asked officials why they chose to go into the field, the most frequent responses were that they loved sport and wanted to stay involved, and that they like the challenge offered by officiating.[5]

Officials are not typically motivated by a sense of glory or financial rewards; rather, they simply want to continue participating in the sporting environment after their athletic careers have ended. In essence, officials find sports intrinsically motivating—and that is the strongest motivation of all.

However, it is easy to have this motivation undermined by hassles that often accompany officiating. When such negative events occur, you need to focus on the idea that officiating is a challenge and being part of sport competition is an exciting and rewarding endeavor. Remember, you play a critical role in facilitating and even ensuring fair and equitable competition. So focus on your original motivations for becoming an official and enjoy the sense of challenge and feeling of accomplishment that officiating can provide.

SUMMARY

If you are not motivated to live up to your officiating potential, then you will probably fall short in becoming a competent official. But staying motivated is not always easy because officials seldom receive much in the way of financial or social rewards.

One effective way to sustain motivation is through goal setting. When correctly set, goals can be tremendously effective tools for increasing motivation and improving performance. Goals should be written down, short-term and long-term in nature, positive, and realistic but challenging. You should identify strategies to meet each goal and develop a program that will enable you to chart your progression toward success. All goals should be under your control and reflect improvements based on personal standards of excellence.

In addition to goals, such things as finding inspiration in models, rewarding yourself, developing a social support network, and nurturing intrinsic motivation will help you maintain your commitment to officiating.

Relaxation
6

Trying to be a successful official is just like preparing for war. You don't know who's going to be the guy who finks out when you come face to face with death.[1]

ANXIETY: A NEGATIVE EMOTION

Officiating is very emotional and stressful. Referees are often targets of unruly crowds, agitated coaches, and belligerent athletes. Although it might sound far-fetched to equate officiating with performing in a battle, officials have been seriously hurt or even killed because of crowd rioting or player aggression. For example, a disputed call at a soccer game in Lima, Peru, in 1964 led to a brawl in which 300 people, including the officials, died. And in 1969, the World Cup play-off series between Honduras and El Salvador turned into ''The Soccer War'' that listed the series' officials among its thousands of casualties. Thus the volatile nature of sport and the burden of keeping athletes', coaches', and fans' emotions in check add to the already stressful task of making judicious calls throughout the competition.

The level of officiating has little to do with the amount of stress experienced. Whether an official is working the seventh game of the World Series, the Super Bowl, or the finals of an intramural tournament, there is pressure to perform unerringly. Making a close call at home plate in the bottom of the ninth inning with the score tied, dealing with an irate coach, coping with an unruly crowd, calling for a penalty shot at the end of a soccer game, and being constantly evaluated by everyone in attendance are just a few situations that put pressure on officials.

Wouldn't you rather deal with these high-pressure situations effectively than become anxious and tentative, perhaps losing control of the game? Coping with stress requires fortitude and conviction, as pointed out by football official Kelly Nutt:

> You can bring your whistle and you can bring your flag, but
> if you don't bring your guts you might as well stay home.[2]

Of course, coping with stressful situations calls for more than self-assurance. And it is not enough to know the rules, regulations, mechanics, and positioning—any of these skills can be interfered with if you become overanxious and "lose your cool." What you need in addition to these qualities are psychological skills that allow you to prevent and manage stress responses to the difficult situations. Having such psychological skills doesn't completely eliminate your feelings of anxiety, but you can learn to manage and channel stress more effectively. Before developing this psychological skill, you must first understand what causes anxiety and how this affects your performance as an official. With a better understanding of the nature of anxiety and its physical and psychological effects on performance, you will learn to control your anxiety and deal with the pressures of officiating in highly competitive sporting environments.

SOURCES OF ANXIETY

Sport participants are often asked to describe the situations and circumstances that make them anxious. One survey[3] asked participants, "What is the one thing that has most prevented you from reaching your potential as an athlete?" The most frequent response was "The failure to effectively cope or deal with my anxieties before and during the competition."

Anxiety plays a similarly critical role in an official's performance during a competition. In fact, a recent survey assessing stress levels of basketball officials revealed that more than 45% of them felt that

their job was either stressful or very stressful.[4] Furthermore, the officials reporting the most stress also reported more physical symptoms
such as headaches, muscle tension, and hypertension.

As noted in chapter 1, a critical attribute of a successful official is
the ability to remain calm and in control despite adverse circumstances.
In essence, great officials are distinguished by their ability to make
the proper calls and take control of the game under pressure. Before
we discuss how to manage your emotions and effectively cope with
the pressures of the job, let's examine the potential sources of stress
that are unique to the official:

- Fear of failure
- Fear of inadequacy
- Perceived loss of control

Fear of Failure

At the core of most officials' anxiety is the fear of failure. In its most
basic form, fear of failure includes worrying about blowing an important call, being out of position, having a bad game, getting a poor
evaluation, or not meeting your own expectations. Survey results
reveal this pervading fear among officials, who reported that being
rated by supervisors and coaches was a major source of anxiety.[5]

Many officials see the evaluation process as a challenge to their egos
and self-esteem. This attitude is clearly revealed at umpire schools,
summer clinics, and referee camps, where officials respond to the stress
and frustration of the evaluation process by feeling embarrassed,
cursing, and even crying. Many officials who suffer such setbacks
determine that they don't have what it takes and silently withdraw
from officiating.

Officials are justified in their concern over coaches' ratings of their
performances. As they note in disgust, coaches' evaluations of them
rarely reflect their actual officiating performance:

- A strong relationship exists between the type of rating received
  and the victory or defeat of the coach's team.
- Ratings are based on specific calls rather than proper mechanics
  and positioning or the quality of the majority of the calls an official
  makes during a given game.
- Coaches are biased; they are too wrapped up in winning to be
  objective in their officiating evaluations.
- One bad night can ruin the whole year. An official can have a
  good rating all season, and, bingo, something unusual can happen
  in the last game that has a devastating effect on his or her
  evaluation.

Officials have a great fear that a poor evaluation by a coach or supervisor, even if unfounded, will have a tremendous negative impact on their reputation. For this reason, many officials dread the evaluation process, even though they admit that it can be useful. But in reality, fears about evaluation (as well as other fears) are usually rooted in each official's deep-seated insecurities. These insecurities dwell within each of us but are much more prevalent in particular individuals under certain circumstances. Officials are not immune to self-doubt, as characterized by the following statements: "I'll never be able to face my peers if I let this game get out of control," and "If I blow a big call, everyone will think I choked under pressure." Such statements suggest that officiating a game takes on greater importance than the outcome of the game itself. Poor performance, or more precisely, the perception of poor personal performance, represents a threat to an official's self-esteem. Somehow, the official comes to believe that "I am a better person and will be well liked if I call a good game, whereas I will be a lesser person and not well liked if I blow some big calls." Thus the ego becomes closely tied to performance.

To further complicate matters, officials know that if they do a good job they will probably go unnoticed, whereas if there is a controversial call, a fight between players, an ejection of a player or coach, or any other unusual happening that requires an official's judgment, the official is usually thrust into the spotlight. Such is the dilemma: To realize the personal satisfaction of a smooth, effective performance, the official must sacrifice being recognized by players, fans, and coaches. Your successes go unappreciated, whereas your failures become highly scrutinized. This dilemma further increases an official's fear of failure.

A good example of this is an event that occurred during the sixth game of the 1985 World Series between the Kansas City Royals and the St. Louis Cardinals. It was the ninth inning, with St. Louis leading 4-3, and Kansas City was at bat. A Royal batter hit a ground ball that resulted in a close call at first base. Umpire Don Denkinger called the runner safe. The call was vehemently argued by the Cardinals and instant replay clearly showed that the runner was out. Kansas City took advantage of the call to rally and win the game. They then went on to defeat St. Louis in Game 7, 11-0. Many Cardinal players blamed Denkinger for their loss, and the umpire took a lot of fan and media abuse over the incident. Despite the thousands of calls Don Denkinger had made in his years of umpiring, his name would forever be linked to this one error he made while in the spotlight.

Obviously, few officials have the opportunity to work a World Series or Super Bowl or to receive the publicity afforded by such "media events." However, an intramural church league, city league, or varsity game is just as important to the athletes and coaches involved. They expect excellent officiating at their level of competition. But such expectations place enormous pressure on officials to perform flawlessly and thereby increase their concern about failing.

Fear of failure causes officials to be tentative in their calls and indecisive in their reactions to critical situations. An official afraid of making a mistake is content to stay in the background and not take control over the game when necessary. If the official's goal is to avoid failure (e.g., making an incorrect call at a crucial point in a game), he or she will dodge important decisions that might affect the outcome of a game. Such a hands-off approach ensures that the official will do what he or she has been trying to avoid: fail.

Fear of Inadequacy

Anxiety also results from a feeling of physical or mental inadequacy for an upcoming event. Fear of inadequacy is specifically characterized by the attitude that "something is wrong with me," an attitude that reflects self-depreciation and personal dissatisfaction. This fear can be based on real or imagined incompetence or a lack of physical or psychological preparation.

Officials may feel ill at ease because of a perceived lack of ability or failure to prepare themselves for an upcoming competition. Officials report feeling inadequate about their inability to

- control tension,
- get in adequate physical condition,
- maintain concentration,
- sustain self-confidence,
- control the game, and
- interpret and apply the rules.

An official must be physically, mentally, and emotionally ready to perform. Good officials try to prevent feelings of inadequacy by preparing themselves for every assignment (see chapter 2). Just as an athlete prepares both mentally and physically for an upcoming opponent, so also should officials prepare themselves to perform well every time out. This preparation includes previewing the contest's players and coaches, anticipating any potential problem areas, staying on a solid exercise training regimen, examining any unique aspects of the competition site, and reviewing the specific rules and regulations that will be in effect for this specific event.

Planning and preparation makes you feel more sure of yourself. Staying in shape is an important part of this process for several reasons, as described by this soccer official:

> It is extremely important for officials to project an athletic image. Officials must be able to maintain the physical pace of the game and must be free to concentrate without being concerned about their stamina. If an official does not project such an image, they open themselves up to additional criticism from coaches, players, and fans. An official's job is difficult enough under normal circumstances; any avenue for unnecessary criticism should be avoided. Respect is gained from coaches, and players by those who work as hard as them to prepare for competition.

And this baseball umpire concurs:

> Athletes must be in tip-top physical shape; officials owe it to the teams involved to project a similar image of top physical and mental alertness. That image is weakened when a referee is overweight and sloppily dressed. An official's credibility is undermined when his or her appearance is in jeopardy and a sense of pride is not evident.

Perceived Loss of Control

Officials also feel anxious about not being in control of the situation. Being in control involves believing that one's actions and efforts will have a direct influence on the outcome of a particular situation. In contrast, a perceived loss of control is associated with feelings of ineffectiveness and impotence. For example, officials report that they feel they've lost control when they are being baited by coaches, working with incompetent officials, or getting criticized in the press. Each of the situations causes them a great deal of stress.[6]

Let's look at some specific situations in which officials feel a loss of control. One such situation involves officiating a game in which there is a coach or player who is known to push officials and create public scenes, such as Indiana University basketball coach Bob Knight or former number-one world-ranked tennis player John McEnroe. Officiating or umpiring in these situations is stressful because these individuals are known for becoming upset over almost every call or decision that is not in their favor. Confrontations between a player or coach and an official can certainly be very trying and stressful for the official. What you and other officials must realize is that, although the coach's or player's behavior may be beyond your control, you can and should control your own behavior and actions. Acting decisively and professionally often diffuses the anger or discontent of an antagonist. If it doesn't, you must take appropriate measures to see that your safety and integrity are protected. It does no good to worry about behavior that is beyond your control.

Officials also feel apprehensive about spectators. Whereas most athletes often play before supportive, enthusiastic crowds, officials rarely ever get a single cheer. In most cases, officials are faced with crowds that range from apathetic to belligerent. Loud booing or derogatory comments from the stands can be intimidating. In extreme cases officials have even been threatened with violent actions, as in the following instance.

An anonymous caller telephoned Milwaukee's Mecca arena during the Bucks-Philadelphia 76ers' game and threatened the life of NBA official Earl Strom. CBS reported the threat during the 4th quarter of the game, which Strom worked with Ed Rush. Although a courtside alternate was available to replace Strom, he safely completed his duties.

Although the behavior of the crowd is, for the most part, out of an official's control, it should not influence or affect your own officiating behavior on the court or field. Once again you need to maintain control over what you do. You should not be concerned with how the crowd reacts, unless it directly affects the continuity of the game itself. Granted, it's hard to ignore 10,000 screaming fans; and it's normal for these types of conditions to make you anxious. But a good official copes with anxious feelings by maintaining control over his or her emotions and the immediate situation.

Although we have described the most prevalent sources of anxiety, it would be impossible to cover all the different situations and circumstances that elicit stress in officials. There are literally as many sources of anxiety in officiating as there are officials. These include working big games, juggling being an official and holding a full-time job, meeting the demands on family life, traveling, and dealing with coaches.

Stress is a very individual experience. But we hope that this discussion of its many sources has given you a clearer understanding of what makes you anxious when you officiate. Now let's examine how such excess anxiety can affect you both physically and psychologically.

HOW ANXIETY IS MANIFESTED

To explain how anxiety negatively influences performance we break down its effects into physical and psychological consequences.

Physical Manifestation of Anxiety

From a physical standpoint, a fight-or-flight response occurs every time an individual is confronted with perceived danger. This response has evolved over thousands of generations, protecting the human species from imminent harm or danger. It is an automatic protective system that is extremely effective in keeping us alive. Here is a brief description of how the fight-or-flight response works.

You recognize a potentially threatening situation. This signals the body to activate the adrenal glands to release several hormones including adrenaline, noradrenaline, and cortisone. These hormones prepare the body and mind for an emergency situation. Heart rate and breathing intensify, and the accompanying panting allows you to quickly eliminate carbon dioxide. The muscles start to tighten. Even the muscles surrounding the lungs begin to tighten, causing shortness of breath and making breathing even more rapid.

This automatic reaction provides energy during threatening situations and enables us to react quickly to danger. Problems arise, however, when the system is activated because of everyday, non-life-threatening events. For example, you may experience this response upon learning that your supervisor will be grading your performance at the upcoming championship game you are scheduled to officiate. The immediate increased heart rate, muscle tension, and release of adrenalin caused by your awareness of the situation will in turn increase your arousal. And if the response continues, you will find it more difficult to perform a number of your officiating tasks effectively throughout the course of the contest.

When we are tense, we tend to contract inappropriate muscles for extended periods of time. Note the tightness you experience in your neck and shoulders after a long workday. These two areas are common sites of excess tension. A major physical problem resulting from this excess anxiety and muscle tension is fatigue. Contracting a muscle for prolonged periods of time eventually tires out the muscle. Officials of fast moving events such as basketball, soccer, and football must be in good physical shape to counteract this fatigue. But even the best conditioned officials will succumb to excessive anxiety, and this adversely affects their performance, if not their health.

Psychological Manifestation of Anxiety

Although excess anxiety negatively affects an official physically, probably of greater concern is the effect of anxiety on the psychological functioning of an official. The two primary areas in which officials experience the psychologically detrimental effects of excess anxiety are reduced concentration and impaired decision making.

Reduced Concentration

Anxiety can be distracting and hamper an official's ability to focus on the important aspects of the game. Anxious individuals are more likely to focus on worries and inner sensations than their job responsibilities.

Suppose that you are officiating an important championship basketball game and intend to do a good job, but at the same time you are nervous and anxious because you lack experience in this type of setting. You happen to be matched with a "big-name" official, and you are anxious not to make any rookie mistakes. As the game begins you are worried about making the right calls and being in proper position. Preoccupied with these thoughts and worries, you miss an important call at a critical juncture of the game because you were focusing on your own insecurities and not on the action. Unfortunately, this scenario is common among officials, particularly when they are placed in a new situation or lack the experience to deal with the pressures inherent to the job.

Impaired Decision Making

A second area of psychological functioning affected by increased anxiety is decision making. An official has the unenviable task of having to make numerous split-second decisions. Some of these decisions are based on specific rules, whereas others involve more judgment. This places a lot of pressure on you to be prompt, precise, and definitive when you blow the whistle. If you are worried or anxious, then your judgment and decision making will invariably be impaired.

Imagine officiating a game in which one of the coaches has a reputation for baiting the referees and putting pressure on them through a variety of antics that excite the hometown crowd. Any call you make against the home team is very unpopular and is greeted by a chorus of boos. As the game progresses you begin to feel anxious, anticipating a confrontation with the coach. Sure enough, a close call goes against the home team and the coach questions the call and pleads with you to change it. Anxious to maintain control of the game, you immediately throw the coach out of the game, which instead sends the crowd and the coach into a frenzy. When you calm down you realize that your apprehension about a possible confrontation with the coach caused you to act hastily and use bad judgment. The proper thing would have been to warn the coach that such a reaction to a call was unacceptable and its recurrence would warrant an ejection. However, at the time, because of your anxiety-affected decision-making process, you were unable to make such a reasoned response.

POSITIVE EMOTIONAL ENERGY

Thus far we have focused our discussion of emotions and performance on the potential debilitating effects of negative emotions. But a lethargic, bored, listless, and uninterested official is going to have an equally hard time performing his or her job effectively and enthusiastically. That is, to be an effective official, you must be energized by positive emotions and feelings.

The positive emotional energy associated with optimum performance is characterized by alertness, energy, enthusiasm, and vigor. In addition, this type of energy is a very pleasant and enjoyable experience. Athletes describe achieving these positive feelings in terms of getting psyched up, pumped up, or high for a performance.

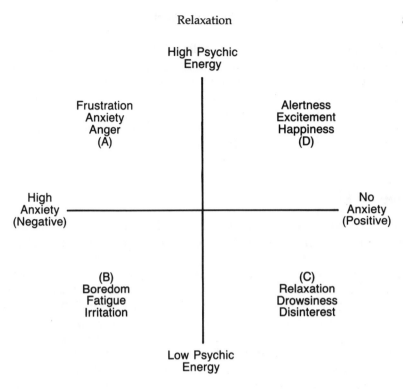

Figure 6.1 The relationship between positive and negative emotions.

Positive and negative emotions are displayed in two dimensions in Figure 6.1. The psychic energy dimension continuum runs from low energy to high energy. The anxiety dimension continuum runs from high anxiety to no anxiety. Quadrant A of the figure represents a combination of high energy and high anxiety, resulting in negative emotional states. An umpire who throws a player out at the slightest provocation may well be operating in a Quadrant A frame of mind. When high levels of anxiety are combined with low levels of energy (Quadrant B), an official will appear agitated but tired. In Quadrant C, where there is no stress and a low energy level, a pleasant feeling of lethargy is common. Finally, when there is no stress but a high level of energy (Quadrant D), an enthusiastic and happy demeanor could be expected.

RELATIONSHIP BETWEEN EMOTIONS AND PERFORMANCE

Now that you are familiar with the concepts of positive and negative emotions, let's look at their practical implications for officiating.

Athletes and coaches have long realized the importance of emotions in optimal performance. They constantly seek the exact "level of intensity" that maximizes performance for a big game or event. Officials, like yourself, also need to be at an optimal emotional level to perform up to their capabilities.

The key question, then, is, What is the optimal level of emotional arousal that will yield your best performance? The answer may be found in the inverted-U principle.

Inverted-U Principle

Research[7,8] has demonstrated that the relationship between emotional arousal and performance can best be described as an inverted-U curve (see Figure 6.2). In its simplest form, the curve suggests that performance will increase as emotional arousal increases up to some optimal level, whereupon further increases in arousal will produce a decrement in performance. Stated another way, performance will suffer when there is too little (underaroused) or too much (overaroused) emotional arousal. And at the top of the inverted-U curve is the optimal level of emotional arousal where performance is maximized.

The inverted-U principle is an outgrowth of common sense. Think of the times when you were so pumped up, aroused, and psyched that you performed poorly; similarly, recall the times when you felt lethargic and passive and, as a result, performed poorly. As an official, your goal should be to consistently reach your optimal level of emotional arousal for every game, regardless of the conditions involved.

To fully understand the inverted-U principle, however, you'll need to refer to the concepts of positive and negative emotional energy. Martens[9] warns that many coaches and athletes misinterpret the inverted-U principle by assuming that peak performance occurs at a moderate level of emotional arousal, regardless of whether that arousal is positive or negative. In fact, research and anecdotal evidence indicates that performers are at their best when they have high levels of positive energy and little or no negative energy.[10]

We have therefore redrawn the inverted-U principle in Figure 6.3. The difference between Figure 6.3 and Figure 6.2 is found on the horizontal axis in the representation of emotional arousal. That is, in the original conceptualization, emotional energy is shown moving along the horizontal axis from low to high, with optimal performance occurring at moderate levels of emotional energy. In the revised inverted-U explanation, emotional energy is differentiated as either positive or negative. The optimal performance area occurs when there is a maximum amount of positive emotional energy and no trace of negative energy.

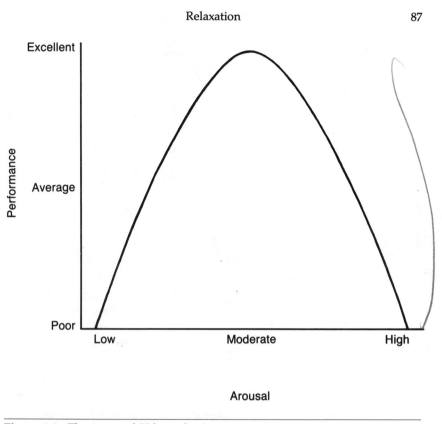

Figure 6.2   The inverted-U hypothesis.

According to Martens'[11] conceptualization of the inverted-U principle, the relationship between positive and negative emotions is the critical performance-determining factor. The challenge is to generate high positive energy while eliminating negative energy. This is not easy, and officials find it particularly difficult to rid themselves of negative emotions such as anxiety, because officiating presents so many stressful situations. Note, however, that you can still perform well even if you experience some negative energy because you can offset it with high positive energy.

Referring to Figure 6.1, you can now see why optimal performance will most consistently occur in Quadrant D, the positive energy cell. In further support of this notion, performers report that peak experiences virtually always occur when they have high positive energy and no negative energy.[12] Emotional states represented in the other three quadrants all typically produce performance that is less than optimal because there is either too much negative energy (Quadrants A and B) or not enough positive energy (Quadrant C).

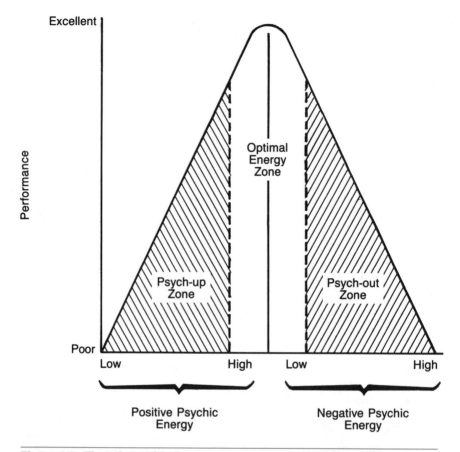

Figure 6.3 The relationship between positive and negative energy and performance.

Individual Differences in Anxiety Performance

Although we have discussed the optimal energy zone as if it applied to everyone in exactly the same way, it is important to note that the optimal energy zone differs for each individual. Some people perform best at relatively low emotional energy levels. You can see these individual differences in Figure 6.4. Although performers A, B, and C all have an inverted-U relationship between emotional energy and performance, they each have a unique optimal energy zone. That is why you should not compare yourself to other officials. Different individuals function differently!

So don't be concerned with how others get themselves emotionally ready, instead, focus on your own optimal state of emotional arousal. The rest of the chapter provides exercises, techniques, and suggestions to help you reach your ideal performance state.

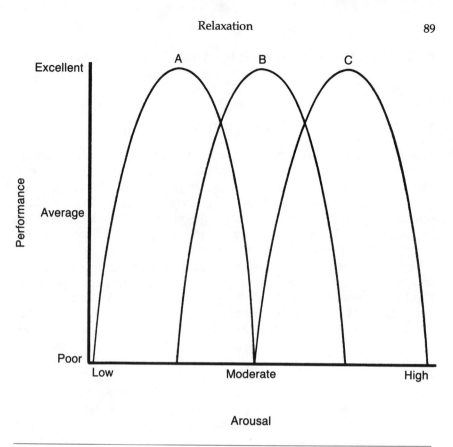

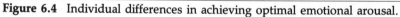

Figure 6.4 Individual differences in achieving optimal emotional arousal.

MANAGING POSITIVE AND NEGATIVE EMOTIONAL STATES

The ability to eliminate or effectively cope with negative emotions is one of the most important steps toward achieving your ideal performance state. As previously discussed, excess anxiety disrupts both physiological and psychological processes.

The Ups and Downs of Officiating

Officials are extremely susceptible to feelings of tension and apprehension. Rarely are they recognized or appreciated for doing a good job, yet they are ridiculed, criticized, and abused when coaches, athletes, fans, or the media think the officials missed a call or called a game poorly. Even if you perform well and make all the right decisions, you'll probably still take some heat if close calls go against the home team. That's why it's important to develop a strategy for coping with the different stressful situations that you will encounter in your job. You can start by developing a keen awareness of your own optimal arousal level.

Self-Awareness of Your Emotional State

The first step in controlling your emotional arousal while officiating is to become more aware of your inner feelings. This involves self-monitoring your feeling states and recognizing how they relate to your performance. You will probably be able to associate certain feeling states with your better performances and other states with your poorer performances. To become more aware of your feeling states, we recommend the following procedures.

Think back to a game in which you really took control of a difficult situation, made your calls decisively, and communicated your decisions confidently and calmly to coaches and players. Try to visualize the game as clearly as possible. Focus on what you were thinking and feeling during this time. Don't rush yourself—take at least 5 minutes to relive this positive officiating experience. Now, complete the items in Table 6.1. For the first item, because you are reconstructing your best performance, you would circle "1." For the second item, if you felt moderately anxious, you would circle "4." There are no right and wrong answers. The purpose of the inventory is to allow you to get a better handle on the relationship between your own mental states and your effectiveness as an official. After doing this for your best performance, do the same thing for your worst performance.

Table 6.1 Checklist of Psychological States

Officiated very well	1	2	3	4	5	6	7	Officiated very poorly
Extremely relaxed	1	2	3	4	5	6	7	Extremely anxious
Extremely confident	1	2	3	4	5	6	7	Not confident at all
Extremely motivated	1	2	3	4	5	6	7	Not motivated at all
Complete control	1	2	3	4	5	6	7	No control at all
Extremely energetic	1	2	3	4	5	6	7	Extremely fatigued
Positive self-talk	1	2	3	4	5	6	7	Negative self-talk
Extremely enjoyable	1	2	3	4	5	6	7	No fun at all
Focused concentration	1	2	3	4	5	6	7	Unfocused
High energy	1	2	3	4	5	6	7	Low energy
Decisive	1	2	3	4	5	6	7	Indecisive

After you have completed this exercise, compare how you responded to the two situations. Most individuals find that their feeling states for their best and worst performances are distinctly different. However, this is just the beginning of your awareness training.

To further develop your self-awareness, make several copies of the inventory (Table 6.1) and monitor your feelings and performance throughout your next several officiating assignments. Complete the inventory as soon as possible after each officiating assignment. Your results probably won't be as extremely high or low as they were in the ideal or worst performance scenarios.

Also, note how your psychological state varies throughout the course of an athletic event. For example, a basketball referee might feel in control, confident, and relaxed for three quarters, only to lose these feelings in the fourth quarter when the game is on the line. If you notice such changes, you might complete an inventory during each intermission of the contest. Remember, this is only an estimate of your feelings, so don't expect absolute precision. However, if you are serious about doing this, you'll be pleasantly surprised how quickly you can enhance your awareness of your mental states.

With this increased awareness, you have a much better chance of consistently reaching your optimal level of arousal. The most important thing to recognize is the relationship between how you feel on the inside and how you perform on the outside. The ultimate objective is to gain a high degree of control over your feelings and thereby control your performance level. The exercises and strategies presented in the remainder of this chapter are designed to help you accomplish this goal.

MANAGING ANXIETY PHYSICALLY AND PSYCHOLOGICALLY

Anxiety management techniques can be broken down into two approaches: physical and mental. In the physical approach, an environmental stimulus (e.g., angry crowd) is hypothesized to cause an increase in an individual's arousal level. This increased arousal might manifest itself through increased heart rate, muscle tension, respiration, sweating, or a number of other autonomic nervous system changes. If you experience anxiety in this manner while officiating, you need to learn a coping technique that will allow you to relax. Then, when you are in the presence of the arousing stimulus (in this case an angry crowd), you can feel relaxed and calm. In essence, physical anxiety management techniques involve learning how to respond to the anxiety-producing event with increased physical relaxation instead of increased arousal.

The other main strategy for reducing anxiety is a mental or cognitive approach. This technique is useful if a stimulus (e.g., the angry crowd) regularly produces negative thoughts, such as "What if I can't control the crowd?" These negative thoughts produce excess anxiety. The mental approach to anxiety management assumes that your perception of the anxiety-producing event, rather than the event itself, is critical. Thus the most effective way to intervene in the anxiety-worry cycle is to change the way you think about the situation. Now that you've been introduced to the rationale for using either physical or mental relaxation management, let's examine the most common techniques used in these two approaches.

Physical Relaxation Techniques

A variety of relaxation techniques attempt to reduce anxiety by decreasing muscle tension and alleviating other associated symptoms of excess anxiety. One of the most effective, yet relatively simple, techniques is breath control.

Breath Control

Breathing is the key to achieving relaxation. In fact, one of the easiest and most effective ways to control anxiety and tension is through proper breathing. Notice how your pattern of breathing is short, forced, and irregular when you are anxious. In contrast, when you are calm, confident, and in control, your breathing is smooth, deep, and rhythmical. Thus you can learn about your mental state just by taking stock of your breathing pattern.

Practicing Breath Control

As with any skill, you must practice breath control to develop it. One technique that performers use regularly and successfully focuses on breathing from the diaphragm instead of the chest. By focusing on the lowering (inhalation) and raising (exhalation) of the diaphragm, you'll experience a greater sense of stability, centeredness, and relaxation. Here is a precise description of this breath control procedure.

Inhalation:
Inhale deeply and slowly through your nose and, as you do, notice how your diaphragm presses downward. Breathe from your stomach and diaphragm and then let the air fill and expand the central and upper chest. Do this in a very easy, relaxed manner. Push your stomach fully outward as you breathe in. This inhalation phase should last approximately 5 seconds.

Exhalation:

Exhale slowly through your mouth in a very relaxed manner. You should feel the muscles in your arms and shoulders relax. As you breathe out and relax, you should begin to feel centered and well anchored to the ground. Your legs should feel relaxed, yet solid and firm. The entire exhalation phase should last roughly 7 seconds. It's important that you exhale slowly and steadily.

Applying Breath Control

You can make use of breath control while officiating a game or event whenever there is a break in the action. The slow, deliberate inhalation-exhalation sequence is one of the best ways to maintain your composure and control over anxiety throughout the course of a game. By focusing on your breathing, you'll be less likely to focus on irrelevant cues such as spectator antics or distracting tirades by coaches or players. Deep breathing will also help relax shoulder and neck muscles and still allow you to feel strong, centered, and ready for action. Because tension is frequently manifested in the shoulder and neck area, this is very important to keeping relaxed and loose.

Your breathing skills can be particularly useful during a time-out, if you are becoming tired, struggling, or feeling tense. This is a good opportunity to pull yourself together. Through deep breathing you

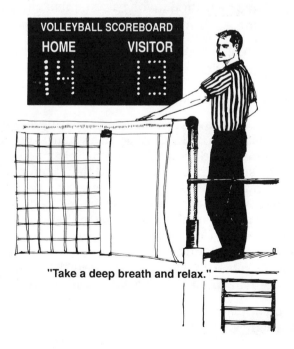

"Take a deep breath and relax."

can calm and slow down the body so you can focus your energies on your assignment. And focused breathing during time-outs allows you to take a short mental break from the pressure of calling the game and reenergize yourself for the rest of the competition.

Progressive Relaxation (Muscle Relaxation)

Progressive relaxation was developed by Dr. Edmund Jacobson in the 1930s,[13] and his technique has formed the cornerstone for modern relaxation procedures. Jacobson called it *progressive* relaxation because the procedure progresses from one muscle group to the next until all the major muscle groups are completely relaxed. The technique has been modified considerably over the years; its purpose, however, is the same: to help individuals learn to feel tension in their muscle and then be able to let go of this tension.

Some of the basic tenets of progressive relaxation include the following:

- It is possible to learn the difference between tension and relaxation.

- Tension and relaxation are mutually exclusive. It is not possible to be relaxed and tense at the same time.

- Progressive relaxation involves systematically relaxing and contracting each major muscle group in the body.

- Relaxation of the body through decreased muscular tension will, in turn, decrease mental tension.

General Progressive Relaxation Instructions

Progressive relaxation involves tensing and relaxing specific muscles. These tension-relaxation cycles develop an awareness of the difference between tension and lack of tension. Each cycle involves maximally contracting one specific muscle group and then attempting to totally relax that same muscle group while focusing on the difference between tension and relaxation. Individuals skillful in this technique are capable of detecting tension in a specific muscle like the neck and then relaxing that muscle. Some even learn how to use the technique during breaks in an activity such as a time-out.

Before you learn how to relax spontaneously, however, you should know about certain conditions that help you to relax.

- Find a quiet place
- Dim the lights

- Loosen any tight-fitting clothing
- Lie down in a comfortable position

Using Progressive Relaxation

Appendix A is a complete description of the progressive relaxation procedure. The first few practice sessions will probably take up to 30 minutes. However, as you learn the progressive relaxation technique you will be able to reduce this time. In fact, within three or four practice sessions, you might be able to relax within 5 to 10 minutes. When you can achieve relaxation regularly within 10 minutes, you can omit the muscle tension component. Remember, the final goal of progressive relaxation is to learn how to completely relax within a short period of time in the midst of a stressful officiating situation.

Mental Relaxation Techniques

We have just discussed two techniques that address the physical components of stress and tension that often accompany officiating a game, match, or event. Another approach to achieving relaxation is to change the way you think about things.

Self-Talk

When you think about things, what you are really doing is talking to yourself. This is called self-talk. We now focus on understanding the nature of self-talk, the problems with self-talk, and some ways for using self-talk positively.

Types of Self-Talk

Anytime you think about something you are talking to yourself. Self-talk becomes an asset when it enhances self-esteem, confidence, and attentional focus and reduces self-doubt and anxiety. Most officials talk to themselves during a contest, although the frequency and content will differ depending on the person and sport involved. Self-talk can be positive if it helps an official to remain calm, stay focused on the present, and forget past mistakes. Negative self-talk detracts from performance because it is inappropriate, irrational, counterproductive, and anxiety-producing.

Your thoughts have a profound impact on your actions, so it is important to control these thoughts as much as possible. When you are officiating, it is not thinking itself that leads to increased anxiety and poor performance, but rather inappropriate or misguided thinking. You can't keep thoughts from entering your head, but you can control how, what, and when you think. Understanding how self-talk works will help you learn the answers to these questions.

How Self-Talk Works

"We are not disturbed by things, but rather the view we take of them."

Epictetus

"There is nothing either good or bad, but thinking makes it so."

Shakespeare

For ages, philosophers, historians, writers, and psychologists have pondered the critical role that our thoughts have on our emotional responses to events. Yet, most of us intuitively feel that the events around us determine our emotional and physical responses. Consider the following example.

You are officiating in the finals of a prestigious basketball tournament for the first time. The game is closely and intensely contested, with both coaches doing a lot of yelling from the bench. You feel that you have done an excellent job of maintaining control and are hesitant to call a technical with the score tied and less than 2 minutes to play. However, the home team's coach has been baiting you throughout the game, trying to get more favorable calls for his team. Finally, you've had all you can take. You turn around to give him a technical, but at the last instant decide just to give him a final warning.

During this exact instant of hesitation, a player on the home team deflects a pass and the ball goes out of bounds. Because you were turned toward the coach, you didn't see the call. And, unfortunately, the other official was not in position to make the call. You have no alternative but to call a jump ball, which the home team controls and it goes on to win the game in the waning seconds. The visiting coach is livid and blames you for taking away his team's chance at a championship. (In fact the films later confirm the ball obviously went off the home team.) After the game you are really mad and upset with yourself for losing your concentration and blowing such an important call. You think to yourself: "What a stupid thing to do in a critical situation. I just blew my chance of ever working a championship game again. There's no reason for me to keep working hard because I obviously don't have what it takes."

Now consider being in the same situation except reacting differently. Instead of putting yourself down, you objectively look at the call and say to yourself, "I realize that I lost my concentration and cool on that one call, but otherwise I did a good job for my first championship game. I just need some more experience, and I need to practice maintaining my concentration throughout the game." Using positive self-talk, you recognize your ability to be a competent referee and vow to continue working at it.

These contrasting reactions to the same situation demonstrate that events, in and of themselves, are not the cause of your emotional reactions. Rather, how you interpret the event determines your response. The relationship between an event, your self-talk, and your response is highlighted by the examples in Table 6.2. As the examples suggest, self-talk plays a pivotal role in an official's reactions to situations (especially adversity) and directly affects future actions and feelings. Thus it is the way you think about an event, rather than the event itself, that actually produces feelings of pressure, tension, and anxiety.

Table 6.2   Process of Self-Talk

Event (environmental change)	Self-talk (perception/evaluation)	Response (emotional, behavioral, physiological)
Negative self-talk examples:		
Missing an important call in a big game	"I'll never make it as an official"	Discouragement, hopelessness
Letting a big-name coach intimidate you	"I just don't have any guts"	Anger, self-doubt, discouragement
Positive self-talk examples:		
Missing an important call in a big game	"I need to maintain my concentration throughout the game"	Optimism, motivation to do better, better concentration
Letting a big-name coach intimidate you	"I know what to expect next time—I'll be better prepared"	Optimism, motivation to do better, better mental preparation

Techniques to Improve Self-Talk

To gain control over your self-talk, you must first become more aware of what you say to yourself. If you're like most officials, you're probably not really in touch with your self-talk, nor do you realize the powerful impact it is having on your performance.

Carefully review the way you use self-talk. Can you identify beneficial and detrimental kinds of self-talk? Are there certain game situations associated with positive and negative self-talk? The important point is to learn how and when to talk to yourself. Two ways to better understand the relationship between self-talk and your officiating performance are through retrospection and self-monitoring.

Retrospection.   Recall your self-talk during previous games or events you officiated. If you have trouble, try to remember some of your best and worst recent performances. Attempt to reconstruct and record the content and frequency of your self-talk in those situations. Most officials notice a distinct difference between the types of self-talk they used in these two situations. That is, officials characterize their better performances as employing positive and instructional self-talk, whereas their poorer performances usually were accompanied by negative self-talk.

Self-Monitoring.   Although referring to past performances is useful, a more accurate way to stay in touch with the nature of your self-talk is through keeping a daily log or journal. Write down your self-talk as soon as you can after officiating each game.

Try to be especially aware of the circumstances that trigger the type of negative, self-destructive statements that create anxiety and impair your effectiveness as an official. Events that typically trigger negative self-talk include the following:

- Blowing a call
- Losing your temper
- Being indecisive
- Losing your concentration
- ''Listening'' to the crowd
- Having a bad game
- Forgetting a rule

Monitoring will undoubtedly make you aware of the crucial role self-talk plays in performance. Once you get a handle on the circumstances and situations that produce negative self-talk, you'll be on your way to becoming a better official. At that point you can begin to change your negative self-statements to positive ones.

Changing Negative Self-Talk to Positive Self-Talk

It would be great if you could eliminate all your negative self-talk. Unfortunately, even the most positive-minded person occasionally allows negative thoughts to intrude. The only way to effectively cope with these negative thoughts is by changing them into positive ones. This reduces your anxiety, redirects your attention, enhances your confidence, and increases your motivation.

One of the best ways to help change your self-talk is to make a list of the kinds of thoughts that upset you and interfere with your officiating performance. With the help of your log, you probably can identify the negative statements and accompanying situations that trigger this type of thinking. And, by recognizing what and when negative self-talk is self-defeating, you can substitute positive statements for negative ones. When you accomplish this task, make up a table with your negative self-talk on one side and your positive self-talk on the other, similar to the arrangement presented in Table 6.3.

Table 6.3 Changing Negative to Positive Self-Talk

Negative self-talk	(change to)	Positive self-talk
That was a terrible call—you idiot.		That's okay, nobody is perfect.
You choked again.		Just relax and do your job.
You just don't have any guts.		Just keep your composure and be decisive.
I'll never be a top-notch official.		I can make it if I just continue to work hard.
What if I can't control the crowd?		Just be confident and decisive—I can do it.
I hate it when I lose my cool.		Take a deep breath and regain control.
I can't work with an incompetent partner.		All I can do is the best that I can.
What will everyone think if I mess up?		I can't worry about what everyone thinks. Just go out and do the job.

Practice changing your self-talk from negative to positive before attempting it during an actual contest. If, like most officials, you have little opportunity to practice your skills in noncontest conditions, you can try two alternatives.

One, try changing your self-talk in situations or games that are seemingly less important to the participants, such as those for recreational leagues. You must take care, however, to continue to do your job, because athletes and coaches at all levels take their sport competition very seriously. They would be upset if they thought you were using their game as a training session.

A second alternative is to use imagery (chapter 8). Imagery is effective for many people and circumvents the problem of using real-life situations for practice. Close your eyes and imagine the specific situation during which you have been troubled by negative self-talk. Once you have visualized the situation and subsequent negative self-talk, try to replace the negative with positive self-talk. (For some typical examples, see Table 6.3.) Do this over and over until it becomes a habit. Once this type of imaging becomes routine, you should be ready to change your self-talk in actual game situations. Although your final goal is to eliminate your negative self-talk altogether, old habits die slowly. Just keep working at it and don't be discouraged if you occasionally fall back on your old habits.

Thought Stopping

Another way of coping with negative thoughts is simply stopping them before they have an adverse affect on your performance. Thought stopping involves concentrating on the undesired thought briefly, then using a cue or trigger to stop the thought and clear your mind.

Because most negative thoughts occur under stress, you should first try to stop the negative thought and then take a deep breath. As you exhale, try to relax and use your trigger to refocus your attention on doing your job effectively. The trigger can be a simple word like ''stop'' or a physical cue such as hitting a hand against a thigh or snapping your fingers. Each person must find the cue that works best for him or her.

To successfully eliminate negative self-talk through thought stopping, you must develop a focused awareness of your thought-producing process. This is not as easy; breaking the bad habit of negative self-talk is as difficult as breaking other bad habits. This is especially true if you have many negative thoughts throughout the course of a game. Eliminating all of these may take some time and effort, so don't expect overnight success. But in ridding yourself of negative thoughts, you will be better able to refocus your attention on the action in the game. To learn the skill of thought stopping, try it during practice or in a low-stress situation. Also, imagine yourself using it before attempting it during an important game.

Tips for On-Site Anxiety Management

Thus far we have described a variety of standard relaxation techniques that can help you manage the anxiety and stress often associated with officiating. You need to practice these systematically until you learn them well enough to use them during actual competitions. Fortunately, you can use a number of tips or cues during the action of a game or event that don't require as much practice. Different techniques work for different individuals, so select the ones that best suit your personality, ability, and sport.

Smile When You Feel Tension Coming On

A simple and effective coping technique is to smile when you feel yourself getting uptight and tense. It is extremely difficult to be mad and upset when you are smiling, and a smile can often take the edge off an upsetting situation. Plus, smiling reminds you to stay in control. You will then realize that it doesn't do any good to get uptight and mad. This allows you to refocus your attention and energies on doing your job.

Prepare for Potential Stressors

One of the best ways to cope with the many stressful situations that typically confront officials is to anticipate and prepare for them beforehand. If you plan in advance for certain types of problems, then you are not likely to be surprised and caught off guard. In addition, you'll be better able to act decisively and effectively without losing your cool. For example, if you are officiating a game involving a coach who has a reputation for baiting and intimidating officials, you could prepare by planning how you will handle the situation. Perhaps you can use imagery to prepare for the coach's reactions to your calls. Try to think of every possible action the coach might take. And be sure always to imagine responding positively and confidently.

Enjoy the Experience

As discussed in chapter 1, it is critical that you enjoy your job. Research[14] shows that enjoyment of participation, whether as a coach, athlete, or official, is one of the key factors to avoiding sport burnout (see chapter 9). One of the main reasons people give for becoming officials is that it allows them to stay involved and to continue to enjoy the sporting experience. In addition, as an official you can enjoy working with young athletes and seeing them improve and grow. Finally, you can derive satisfaction from doing a good job of officiating and take pride in the contribution you make to sport.

Use Cue Words

Words such as "easy," "relax," or "calm" can help you stay relaxed and keep your emotions under control. Cue words are effective reminders to yourself to relax when the pressure starts to build and you feel yourself becoming uptight.

Focus on the Action

This simple method is very effective in dealing with anxiety-producing situations. When you think about what just happened or what might happen, usually your anxiety increases and your concentration suffers. For example, your anxiety will increase if you continue to worry about a call you missed 5 minutes ago. There is nothing you can do about the call—nobody is perfect. Stay focused on the action and don't become distracted by past or future thoughts. Keeping your mind on the present is a critical skill for officiating and one that we will discuss more fully in chapter 7.

Slow Down

Individuals under pressure tend to rush their actions. In the heat of a contest, it's easy to get carried away and make a rash decision that you will regret later. Although in chapter 1 we listed decisiveness as one of the qualities of a good official, it is sometimes beneficial to pause before making a decision. For example, you might reconsider before ejecting a mouthy coach or player from a championship game. That is not to say that you should take verbal abuse from the participants. However, remember that your goal is to stay in the background and let the athletes determine the outcome of the competition. In this case, you might warn the coach or player that "that's enough" or simply ignore him or her.

SUMMARY

This chapter began with an explanation of how and why positive and negative emotional states can affect your performance. Excess anxiety is the prime cause of negative energy. When pressure gets too high, it results in a variety of mental and physical breakdowns, which disrupt your performance and take the fun out of officiating. The key is to generate feelings associated with positive emotional energy while eliminating excess anxiety. This is particularly difficult to do as an official, because so many different stressors come with the job.

The remainder of the chapter described a number of different strategies and techniques for coping with the pressure and stress associated with officiating. The first step is to identify what situations and circumstances cause you to become anxious. You then need to select a relaxation procedure that makes you feel most comfortable. Choose the physical, mental, or combined technique that will work best for your own personal situation. You should practice the technique before applying it in a game, because staying cool, calm, and collected in the face of adverse circumstances is not easy. But learning to cope effectively with these pressure situations will give you a sense of control and self-confidence.

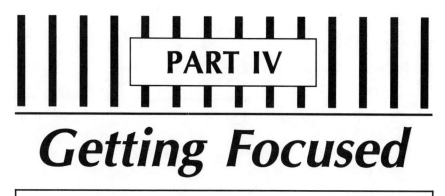

PART IV

Getting Focused

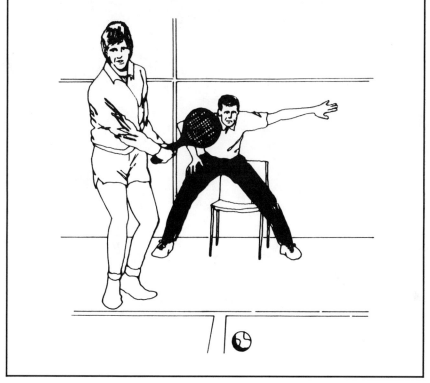

Concentration
7

The most important thing for me when I officiate a game is to maintain my concentration throughout the course of the contest. The old adage that it's a "game of inches" can often be true, and I want to make sure that I'm there and ready to make the call if the situation arises. A lapse in concentration can result in missing a key play which may help determine the outcome of a game. I always want the players to determine who wins and loses. I work hard all the time to keep up my concentration regardless of the game score or level of competition involved.

This volleyball official's statement highlights the critical role that concentration plays in officiating. Many officials think that concentration can be turned on and off like a water faucet. Some believe that when they really need to concentrate they can automatically turn it on and get immediately involved with the action. Others think that if the score is lopsided or the quality of play is poor their full undivided concentration is not necessary. Nothing, however, could be further from the truth. These attitudes cheat not only the players and coaches, but also the official who subscribes to them. This does not mean that officials shouldn't take a mental break during a time-out or other break in the action. Rather, it emphasizes that you need to continuously maintain your concentration throughout the game.

Concentration is a psychological skill that can be learned and refined. To develop good concentration skills, you must practice getting and maintaining the proper attentional focus throughout the contest every time you officiate a game. We suggest ways for you to improve your concentration skills later in the chapter, but first we need to discuss what concentration actually entails.

DEFINITION OF CONCENTRATION

Concentration can be defined in several different ways. In sport psychology, however, concentration is most often defined as *the ability to focus on the relevant cues in the environment and to maintain that focus over the course of the contest*. A closer look at this definition will provide you with a better understanding of the critical role concentration plays in effective officiating.

The first part of the definition refers to focusing on the most important cues in the competitive environment. We can't tell you exactly what to focus on. That is largely determined by your sport and your specific responsibilities within that sport. For example, in baseball, the plate umpire has a different set of responsibilities than the second base umpire, and thus they each have a different attentional focus.

Despite the specific requirements particular to each sport, all officials need to focus on the action and be sensitive to the relevant cues that dictate exactly what aspects of the activity they should focus on. Although it would seem relatively easy to focus on the action in the game, inevitably a wide variety of irrelevant cues compete for your attention. These include antics of the coaches, a hostile crowd, a complaining athlete, thoughts about the outcome of the game, and previously missed calls. As a result, it is important for officials to keep their minds free of these irrelevant thoughts so they can focus their concentration on the action. A college soccer official told us how he avoids becoming distracted:

> When the game gets under way I just try to block out all my thoughts that are not related to the game. I am only interested in doing my job in an effective and efficient manner. When I am doing my job well, it's like I have tunnel vision as I can focus solely on the players and the field. I am not distracted

by the crowd and in fact I sometimes don't even hear them.
I have only one thing on my mind and that is to focus on the
action and call them as I see them.

One of the qualities of a good official is consistency (chapter 1). Being consistent means not only keeping your calls consistent within games but also performing at a consistently high level game after game. Top-flight officials are like elite athletes: Both are able to consistently perform up to their potential. A bad game happens seldom, if at all. A key to developing this consistency is the ability to focus your attention on the relevant cues in the sport that you officiate.

The second part of the definition of concentration refers to the ability to maintain your focus over a period of time. Although it is important to selectively attend to the proper cues, you must also be able to maintain this focus throughout the course of the athletic event. Many sporting events take 2 to 3 hours to complete. And, over the course of a long contest, mental and physical fatigue can set in. When this happens, it is very easy to lose concentration and make a mistake. Keeping the mind on track and alert for long periods of time is difficult, but if you want to be a superior official, you must learn how to stay sharp throughout an entire game.

MAINTAINING CONCENTRATION: AN ATTENTIONAL PROBLEM

To understand why it is so difficult to maintain concentration over extended periods of time you need to understand both how the mind works and the specific nature of sport competition.

Attentional focus is primarily dependent on motivation and the intensity or importance of different stimuli in the environment. For example, if you were home watching a television program in which there was a scene of a fire, you might or might not pay attention. But, if a neighbor came to your door frantically yelling "Fire, fire, fire!", you would most likely forget about the television program and heed your neighbor's warning.

This principle also holds true for officiating. The more intense or important the stimuli (e.g., a championship baseball game in the bottom of the ninth with the score tied 2-2), the less motivation you need to maintain your concentration. Conversely, the less intense or important the stimuli (e.g., the first quarter of an exhibition pee wee football game), the more motivation you need to sustain your concentration.

The interplay between motivation and concentration is captured by the comments of a veteran college basketball official:

> Staying interested in a game from an official's standpoint is a lot harder than many people think. It's sometimes hard to stay motivated and focused when the game is lopsided or of seemingly little importance in terms of team standings. I would have to fight really hard to keep my mind from wandering. It was sometimes a little scary when I realized that I wasn't giving the game my full attention and thus missed a call. But I have come to realize that every game is important and that I owe it to the athletes to be at my best throughout the game.

Officiating different sports requires using different attentional skills. For example, sports that are fairly continuous such as basketball, soccer, and hockey require the ability to concentrate and to keep moving to maintain proper position over extended time periods. Other sports such as wrestling, weight lifting, and swimming are characterized by short but intense competition periods. And sports such as football, baseball, volleyball, and tennis are characterized by a lot of starts and stops in the action. Therefore, an official must tailor his or her attentional capacity to the nature of the sport. The following section describes factors that you should consider when attempting to adjust your attentional focus.

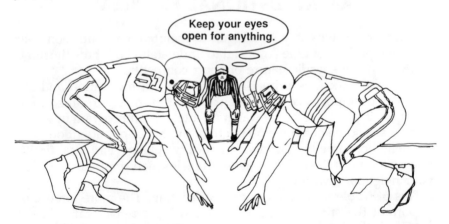

Keep your eyes open for anything.

DIFFERENT TYPES OF ATTENTION

Although every sport has unique cues that you need to attend to, all types of sports have two common characteristics in their attentional demands. Regardless of the activity, the attention required will vary in both *width* and *direction*.

Width of Attention ✶

Width of attentional focus varies along a continuum from *broad* to *narrow.* Certain sports require a fairly broad focus of attention; participants must be sensitive to a variety of cues. A quarterback, for example, must read the defense and still be able to spot an open receiver. Similarly, a soccer official must have a broad perspective so that he or she can scan a large playing area. Likewise, a hockey official needs a broad perspective because the action is continuously changing.

In contrast, a narrow attention is more appropriate for athletes in sports like golf and tennis. And, in officiating, a narrow focus is often required for discriminating judgments. Officials who must use a narrow focus include a tennis chair umpire calling lines, a volleyball official determining if a player touched the net, and a football official deciding whether a receiver was in or out of bounds when catching a pass.

Direction of Attention ✶

Attention also varies in its direction, ranging from *internal* to *external.* Internal attentional focus refers to focusing attention on your own thoughts and feelings, such as "I need to call this game closely to discourage overly aggressive play that might lead to a fight."

Externally focused attention is centered on the events occurring in the environment. External focus is beneficial to an official who must determine where contact was made on a block or a spike in volleyball or whether the ball was on its downward flight on a goaltending call in basketball.

Table 7.1 presents the four different types of attentional focus possible when both the width and direction of attention are considered.

Table 7.1   Four Different Types of Attentional Focus

		Direction of attention	
		External	Internal
Width of Attention	Broad	Broad-external Used to rapidly assess a situation	Broad-internal Used to analyze and plan
	Narrow	Narrow-external Used to focus exclusively on one or two external cues	Narrow-internal Used to mentally rehearse for an upcoming game or control an emotional state

Some sports require a particular type of attentional focus most of the time, but officials must be able to shift their attentional focus quickly. This is not always easy, but it can be done. Rapidly changing your attentional focus requires effectively controlling the width and direction of your attention. Let's now look at an example of how to do this during the course of a game.

As batting practice has ended and the coaches are getting ready to give you, the home plate umpire, their starting lineups, you make some mental notes concerning the specific rules that apply to this field along with how you will be communicating with the other umpires and coordinating your decisions with theirs. You can best make use of this broad internal focus when you have to think about and plan your reactions to new and complex situations. You change to a broad external focus as you take a look around to inspect the conditions of the field to see if the other umpires, coaches, and players are ready to start the game. The home team takes the field and you take a deep breath and tell yourself to relax because you have a tendency to get too uptight. You often use this narrow internal focus to control your emotional states. Finally, as the pitcher delivers the first pitch, you switch to a narrow external focus to determine whether it is a ball or a strike.

FOCUSING ATTENTION INAPPROPRIATELY

One of the keys to good concentration is the ability to change attentional focus at appropriate times while maintaining a particular focus at other times.

But achieving and maintaining proper attentional focus throughout a competitive event is often difficult. The mind has a natural tendency to wander, and officials face numerous potential distractions, both internal and external. Being aware of your attentional problems is the first step toward developing a plan to overcome them. So let's examine the typical problems officials have in focusing and maintaining their concentration.

Thinking About Past Events

Officials frequently are unable to forget previous calls they have made. Yet, focusing on a prior call can hamper an official's performance for the remainder of the game. Here's an example of how attending to past events or calls can wreak havoc on your concentration:

Imagine that you are the chair umpire of a championship tennis match. It is set point. At the end of a long rally, a ball hits near the line. You didn't get a good view of it because your vision was obstructed. Therefore you have to call the ball good. The player goes on to lose this important point, and thus the first set. The player then vehemently protests to you. The crowd's loud booing makes it more evident that they disagreed with your call. You really can't change your call because you didn't see the ball. This makes the player even more angry. You know you probably made a mistake. As the next set progresses, you become preoccupied with this call because it occurred at such a critical point in the match. As a result, you are not really focused on the action of the match. In fact, you find yourself fighting the temptation to even things up.

In this example you suffered a lapse in concentration because you couldn't forget an earlier, controversial play. Therefore, you had an internal focus rather than the external focus needed for the match. Remember, you'll never keep up with the present action if you keep trying to make up for the past. So, acknowledge your mistake (to others, when appropriate) immediately, forget it, and get focused on the contest to see that it doesn't happen again.

Thinking About the Future

Just as thinking about past calls can produce inappropriate focus of attention, so too can focusing on future events. Future-oriented thinking is usually characterized by focusing on the consequences of certain actions. Much of this type of thinking involves self-statements that begin with "what if." Some typical officiating "what ifs" include the following:

What if I blow a big call?

What if the crowd gets out of hand?

What if I don't know a rule?

What if I am unsure about a call?

What if I disagree with the other official?

All of these "what if" questions are irrelevant to the matters you should be concentrating on. Pondering what might happen if you miss

a critical call will only detract from your present concentration. And thinking ahead can be especially troublesome if you do it while the game is going on.

Certainly, this is not to suggest that you should not anticipate certain events during a contest. Indeed, a good official prepares in advance for different situations and circumstances. However, most of this preparation should occur before the game ever begins. Your attention needs to be focused on the action once the game starts. You owe it to yourself and the players to stay in the present and keep focused throughout the game.

Thinking of Too Many Things

Besides thinking into the future or the past, another potential problem is attending to too many cues. This is particularly a problem for officials who have a broad external attentional style because they have a tendency to pay attention to things other than the game.

For an official, spectators are a major source of distraction; they are part of the event and you can't physically eliminate them. Spectators can affect you in several ways. A boisterous home crowd can influence your calls unless you really concentrate on what you're doing. When spectators are cheering loudly for the home team, it is difficult not to be subtly influenced— especially when a call in favor of the home team produces cheers and a call against the home team prompts boos. And, it is only normal to prefer to hear cheers rather than boos directed toward you. Consequently, you must try to block out the crowd noise and just concentrate on doing your job well.

Although spectators are a major source of distraction, as an official you are exposed to many things that can disrupt concentration. In fact, the list of potential distractions is endless.

For example, another game or activity might be going on close to the game you are officiating. Or, the weather might be extremely hot or cold. And because you'll usually have little or no control over such factors, it becomes all the more important that you know how to effectively cope with them. Later in the chapter, we present some specific exercises and techniques that you can use to deal with these distractions.

RELATIONSHIP BETWEEN ANXIETY AND ATTENTION

We have to this point discussed anxiety and attention as separate factors that can influence your effectiveness as an official. However, these two concepts are very much related, and their interplay can have important implications for your performance. In fact, it is really only possible to understand how anxiety affects performance if you are also aware of how anxiety interacts with attentional focus.

Increased anxiety affects both the width and the direction of attentional focus in three different but related ways.

- As anxiety increases, the *width of your attention becomes narrower*. Rather than seeing all the important events happening in the game, you restrict your attention to only a narrow aspect of play. Although a narrow focus is obviously important for an official, too narrow a focus causes you to miss relevant cues and negatively affect your performance. For example, focusing exclusively on the volleyball player who is spiking might result in overlooking the fact that another player has touched the net.

- Excess anxiety also causes you to *focus attention internally*. An internal focus is fine when you are getting ready for a game, but it is problematic when you should be predominantly externally focused on the action of the game. Thinking too much, especially when your thoughts are focused on your own anxieties and worries, will result in "paralysis by analysis" and thus reduce your effectiveness.

- Anxiety affects concentration by *limiting the ability to shift attentional focus*. We have discussed the importance of being able to shift from a broad to narrow and an internal to external focus of attention depending on the situation and type of sport. For example, a soccer referee must constantly and quickly change from a broad to a narrow focus and back as the action moves swiftly up and down the field. But when pressure mounts, typically automatic attentional shifts are more difficult. And, when anxiety is high, both the width and the direction of your attention become less flexible. Thus you might find yourself locked into an inappropriate attentional focus.

Excess Anxiety + Inappropriate Attention = Choking

The interaction between increased anxiety and inappropriate direction and width of attentional focus is the technical way of saying that a person has "choked." Everyone involved in athletics is familiar with the term but few people really know that choking refers to more than performing poorly under pressure. In reality, choking involves a complex interplay of anxiety levels and attentional focus.

Officials choke just as players do, although it may not be as evident to the casual observer. But, the relaxation exercises presented in chapter 6 and the concentration techniques we now describe can help you keep from choking in future officiating assignments.

IMPROVING CONCENTRATION

We have defined concentration as the ability to focus attention on proper cues in the environment and maintain that focus. As in learning to cope with pressure, you must practice your attentional control to systematically develop your concentration skills.

Paradoxically, trying to concentrate is not necessarily the best approach either. Concentration is usually best achieved when you don't try to force it to happen. But, although the act of concentrating is passive, it can only be achieved through active preparation on your part. In preparing to concentrate, you must learn how to

4 keys to improve concentration

- cope effectively with pressure and anxiety;
- selectively attend to relevant cues while ignoring irrelevant ones;
- rapidly refocus attention on your immediate task if distracted; and
- properly employ the rules, mechanics, and positioning to officiate your sport.

Testing Your Ability to Concentrate

You can become more aware of your concentration skills by completing the Self-Help Test (7.1). This test will give you a rough idea of how well you concentrate and whether this is an area you need to improve in to become a better official.

Self-Help Test 7.1
Concentration Skills

The following questions refer to your ability to concentrate while officiating. There are no right or wrong answers. Just write the number that best describes you for each statement.

1 = *Almost never*   4 = *Frequently*
2 = *Rarely*   5 = *Almost always*
3 = *Sometimes*

(Cont.)

Self-Help Test 7.1 (Continued)

_____ 1. If I blow a call, I have difficulty putting it out of my mind.

_____ 2. When I officiate, I am good at quickly analyzing what's happening in the game.

_____ 3. It is easy for me to keep irrelevant thoughts from entering my mind when I am officiating.

_____ 4. I am good at blocking out the noise of spectators and focusing on the action.

_____ 5. While officiating, I get confused when many things happen quickly.

_____ 6. When I officiate, I find myself distracted by my own thoughts.

_____ 7. I am good at analyzing what I need to focus on during an event.

_____ 8. When officiating, I focus on the moment and don't think about what has happened or might happen.

_____ 9. I can maintain my concentration, even during hassles with coaches and players.

_____ 10. I am good at analyzing what I need to do before starting an officiating assignment.

_____ 11. When officiating, I can focus on my assignment and forget all my other problems.

_____ 12. When officiating, I can keep my concentration, even when I get anxious.

_____ 13. When officiating, I can keep my concentration even when my fellow official is doing a poor job.

_____ 14. When officiating, I have no trouble staying focused on the action during the entire event.

_____ 15. After a break in the action, I have trouble regaining my concentration.

Now, using the scoring guidelines found below, add up your total score on the test. Then refer to the rating chart to determine your level of concentration.

Scoring Guidelines: Regular items are scored 1, 2, 3, 4, 5
                      Reversed items are scored 5, 4, 3, 2, 1
                      Reversed items: 1, 5, 6, 15

Rating Chart: Total Score	Rating of Concentration Skill
75-70	Zeroed in
69-60	Need some target practice
59-50	Must find the target
49-40	In the twilight zone
40 and below	Zoned out

The highest possible score is 75 and the lowest is 15. The closer you are to 75 the better your concentration skills. If you scored less than 60, you need to work on your concentration skills. And, even if you score pretty high, there may still be some specific areas you need to develop.

Now that you have a sense of your level of concentration skills, you are ready to begin exercises to improve this skill. The remainder of this chapter presents a variety of on-site and at-home strategies, techniques, and exercises to further develop your concentration skills. Choose the ones that work best for you and for your particular sport.

Exercises to Improve Concentration

Several techniques are available for you to increase your concentration skills. A four-step exercise developed by Gauron[1] is effective in enhancing self-awareness of attentional focus and thus improving your ability to concentrate.

Exercise #1: Learning How to Shift Attention

You may practice this exercise in its entirety or break it down into separate exercises. Before starting the exercises, sit or lie down in a comfortable position and take a few deep breaths from the diaphragm. Begin the technique when you are relaxed and comfortable.

1. Pay attention to what you hear. Take each separate sound and label it, such as voices, footsteps, or the radio. Next, listen to all the sounds around you without attempting to label or classify them. Simply listen to the blend of sounds as if you were listening to music and dismiss all other thoughts.
2. Now become aware of your bodily sensations, such as the feeling of the chair or bed supporting your body. Mentally label each sensation as you notice it. Before moving on to another sensation, let each sensation linger for a moment while you examine

it closely, considering its quality and source. Finally, attempt to experience all of these sensations simultaneously without trying to label any of them. This will require a broad internal focus.

✓ 3. Turn your attention to your own thoughts and emotions. Let each emotion or thought just arise; do not try to specifically think about anything. Remain relaxed and at ease, no matter what you are thinking and feeling. Now try to experience each of your feelings and thoughts one at a time. Finally, see if you can just let go of all these thoughts and emotions and relax.

✓ 4. Open your eyes and pick some object across the room and directly in front of you. While looking straight ahead, see as much of the room and the objects in the room as your peripheral vision will allow. Simultaneously observe the entire room and all the things in it. Now try to narrow your focus of attention to just the object centered in front of you. You should continue to narrow your focus until that is the only object in view. Now expand your focus little by little, widening your perspective until you can eventually see everything in the room. Think of your external focus as a zoom lens; practice zooming in and out, narrowing or broadening your attentional focus according to your preference.

This exercise helps you to experience different attentional styles by shifting your focus across the internal-external and broad-narrow dimensions. This procedure also demonstrates why different types of attention are required to effectively perform the various skills associated with officiating.

Exercise #2: Learning How to Maintain Focus

This exercise will help you focus your attention and maintain that focus.

✓ Find a quiet place where there are no distractions. Choose an object to focus on. It might be beneficial to choose something relevant to the sport or sports you officiate such as a tennis ball, baseball, football, basketball, soccer ball, or volleyball. Hold the object in your hands. Get a good sense of how it feels, its texture, color, and any other distinguishing characteristics. Now put the object down and try to focus your attention on it. Examine it in great detail. If your thoughts wander, bring your attention back to the object.

Record how long you can maintain your focus on the object. You'll find that it's not that easy to stay focused on one object, but that is often what is required of you as an official. Once you are able to focus your attention and stay focused for at least 5 minutes, start practicing with distractions present. Chart how long you can maintain your focus of attention under these conditions. You'll be a better official if you become proficient at maintaining your concentration despite distractions and disruptions.

Exercise #3: Searching for Relevant Cues

One technique that has been commonly used by athletes to increase concentration is known as the grid exercise. This exercise has been used extensively in Eastern Europe as a precompetition screening device. It can give you a sense of what it means to be totally focused at a given point in time.

The exercise requires a block grid containing two-digit numbers ranging from 00 to 99 (see Table 7.2). The object is to scan the grid and within a given period of time (usually 1 minute) put a slash through as many consecutive numbers as possible starting with 00. You can use the same grid several times by simply starting with a higher number than in your previous attempt (e.g., 27, 34, 46, etc.). In addition, you can make new grids by using any combination of numbers. Individuals who have the ability to really concentrate and scan for relevant cues will usually find 25 or more consecutive numbers in 1 minute.

Besides helping you learn to focus your attention and scan the environment for relevant cues (which is particularly important for officials in a fast-moving sport such as soccer and basketball), you can modify this exercise to deal with different situations. For instance,

Table 7.2 Concentration Grid Exercise

42	32	39	34	99	19	64	44	03	77
97	37	92	18	90	53	04	72	51	65
40	95	33	86	45	81	67	13	59	58
78	69	57	68	87	05	79	15	28	36
26	09	62	89	91	47	52	61	64	29
00	60	75	02	22	08	74	17	16	12
25	76	48	71	70	83	06	49	41	07
31	10	98	96	11	63	56	66	50	24
01	20	54	82	46	38	14	94	23	73
88	43	30	85	27	80	21	55	93	35

you can add different types of distractions such as people talking, loud music, or other loud noises. As your concentration improves you will be better able to block out such distractions and focus exclusively on the task. This, in turn, will help you block out distractions and stay completely absorbed in the game.

Exercise #4: Rehearsing Game Concentration

Another way to practice your concentration skills is through the use of imagery or mental rehearsal (see chapter 8). This might involve visualizing an upcoming assignment during which you are reacting efficiently and decisively to a number of different situations or simply making decisions that typically confront you in that sport. For example, a tennis umpire might see a number of shots hit close to the line and decisively make a call. Similarly, a football referee might picture making calls on a number of pass plays in which both offensive and defensive players make contact just as the ball is arriving. The number of situations and calls are endless; only you can decide which ones you want to concentrate on. To make this more difficult, practice visualizing scenes with distractions present and see if you can maintain your focus.

Tips for Better On-Site Concentration

You can do several things to improve your concentration while you are actually officiating. These little tips can be very useful when you encounter situations with extreme attentional demands that often lead to an inappropriate focus of attention:

- Use trigger words
- Focus on the present
- Think noncritically
- Establish routines

Use Trigger Words

You can use simple cue words throughout a game to trigger the desired response. These word can have an instructional component (e.g., "keep low," "position," "focus"), or they can be more emotional or motivational (e.g., "relax," "move," "calm"). Such cues help to center attention on the most appropriate aspects of the game while protecting against intruding thoughts and feelings. Cues should focus on the positive (i.e., what to do) rather than on the negative (i.e., what not to do). For example, tell yourself, "relax," rather than "don't get uptight."

A cue needs to be meaningful to help focus attention on the specific response that promotes concentration. If you notice your concentration slipping, then cue yourself to get back into the flow of the action. The following describes how one official uses cues to help his movement while officiating a football game:

> If I can get into the flow of the game then everything seems to fall into place. For me, this usually means moving well since football requires a lot of movement up and down the field. So I just use the simple word "move" and this seems to trigger my mind and body to get involved and into the game.

Focus on the Present

As mentioned previously, two typical problems in maintaining proper attentional focus are thinking in the past and in the future. Sometimes your mind is so open to incoming messages that it's hard to stay focused on the present. But the importance of staying in the present cannot be overemphasized.

Staying in the present requires a focused concentration throughout the entire competitive event. The mind tends to drift, especially during breaks in the action. It's okay to occasionally take a brief mental break. Even during time-outs, however, you need to stay involved

in the contest and fulfill certain responsibilities. So don't use a pause
in the action to make postgame social plans. Also, if you are officiating
a game played outdoors like soccer, baseball, or tennis, there may be
other activities going on in the vicinity of the game you are working.
Don't give in to the temptation to get a peek of what's happening
in another area. Perhaps when you feel the urge to sneak a look you
can instead, with the help of a cue word (e.g., "focus"), keep your
attention centered on the contest you are working.

Thinking Noncritically

Evaluating your officiating performance from call to call is a definite
threat to your concentration. Evaluating each of your calls will interfere
with your concentration on the action around you.

Furthermore, after you judge a couple of calls or decisions as bad,
it is easy to start generalizing. This can result in self-defeating thoughts,
such as "I always miss the big calls," "I just can't control a game,"
or "I don't have what it takes to be an official." This kind of thinking
inevitably leads to self-doubt, increased anxiety, and a lack of self-
confidence. Therefore, it is important that you look at your performance in a neutral, nonjudgmental way.

This does not mean that you should ignore errors; but you should
review your calls without adding any evaluation or judgment. Maybe
you need to be in better position or to be more decisive on a close
call. Whatever, the case, you gain nothing by attacking yourself. So,
make positive use of your performance evaluation. This will likely lead
to improved performance, and you'll probably find officiating a more
enjoyable experience as well.

Establish Routines

To further minimize distractions and help focus concentration, develop
a consistent routine when officiating. Routines will also help you deal
more effectively with anxiety-producing situations. Athletes use routines or rituals regularly during practices, warm-ups, and actual competitions. What some observers might call superstitious behavior is in
reality just another way for athletes to feel in control of the situation.

Similarly, you can develop routines in preparing to officiate a game
or during the game, especially when there are breaks in the action.
A pregame routine should help narrow your focus of attention and
help you relax as the event draws nearer (see chapter 2). Routines
can also help you stay focused during time-outs and other breaks in
the action. For example, a couple of deep breaths followed by a special
cue word such as "focus" might help you stay calm while keeping

you involved in the game. Routines can vary from extremely simple to very involved. Decide what approach is best and use it consistently every game.

SUMMARY

This chapter discussed the important role that concentration plays in helping the performance of officials. Concentration refers to focusing on the important and relevant cues and maintaining that focus over the course of the competition. We discussed different types of attentional focus including the dimensions of width (broad-narrow) and direction (internal-external). We identified common distractions including focusing on past and future events and attending to too many things. We discussed the result of the interaction between anxiety and attention, what is commonly called "choking."

A variety of strategies and exercises for improving concentration exist for coping with the many distractions officials encounter. These include strategies you can use on-site as well as those you can practice at home. You should select and practice the concentration exercises that feel most comfortable and appropriate for you. And we encourage you to come up with some additional exercises that specifically address the areas of concentration in which you need the most improvement.

Imagery
8

Officials generally do not get to practice their skills the way athletes do. We just can't go and shoot some baskets, hit some golf balls, or practice our tennis strokes. So how I get ready for a game is to imagine different plays, situations, and circumstances; and then I see myself making the call. If I don't like the decision I made, then I replay the same situation again in my mind until I am comfortable with the decision. By doing this I feel confident that I am prepared for the game since I have gone over things in my mind already.

Sport participants have come to believe that rehearsing mentally for an upcoming event enhances subsequent athletic performance. And, according to this particular high school basketball and football official, mental rehearsal can increase a performer's self-confidence.

Athletes have long recognized the benefits of rehearsing or visualizing their upcoming performance. Books are filled with testimonials of sport performers regarding their use of mental rehearsal. For example, in his book *Golf My Way*, golf legend Jack Nicklaus, who won the Master's at age 45, describes in detail his use of imagery before every shot.

> First I "see" the ball where I want it to finish, nice and white and sitting up high on the bright green grass. Then . . . I "see" the ball going there: its path, trajectory, and shape, even its behavior on landing. . . . the next scene shows me making the kind of swing that will turn the previous images into reality.[1]

Although many people have been using imagery for a long time, only recently have researchers recognized its potential for improving performance. The consensus is that mental rehearsal should be a standard part of practice if a sport participant is to perform up to his or her potential. This is especially relevant for officials, who rarely have the opportunity to practice their skills outside a contest. Therefore, imagery skills are an invaluable asset for improving your officiating. This chapter explains what imagery is, how imagery works, and how it can be used to enhance officiating performance, and it helps you set up your own imagery program.

UNDERSTANDING IMAGERY

Imagery refers to reliving or creating an experience in your mind. Thus, even when you're not actually officiating a game, imagery enables you to experience it vividly in your mind. This mind exercise is also referred to as visualization, mental rehearsal, mental practice, and psycho-cybernetics. These techniques all entail a full sensory experience (primarily seeing, feeling, hearing) in the absence of external stimuli.

You've probably already used imagery without even making a systematic effort to do so. For example, have you ever watched professional officials and then tried to imitate their performance in your mind? Or have you ever recalled a particularly good performance and then tried to recreate that feeling or experience in your mind? Imagery is possible because the human mind can remember events and recreate a picture of them.

Similarly, your mind can create or picture new events that have not yet occurred. For example, the official quoted at the beginning of this chapter spoke of trying to create a mental picture of the game that he was about to work.

An alternative is to create situations and circumstances similar to those that have created problems for you in the past. For example, a soccer referee who has been inconsistent in calling fouls might visualize herself correctly and decisively citing players for various violations. Similarly, a hockey referee who has had difficulty in dealing with certain argumentative players might see himself acting in a calm yet firm manner in these situations. As these effective performances go through your mind, you'll notice feeling more confident about your calls during the game. By mentally rehearsing how to deal with particularly difficult situations, you can face them with greater confidence and deal with them more effectively.

Although sight is usually the dominant sense, imagery involves much more than simply visualizing yourself performing an activity. Imagery involves all of the senses. In addition to the *visual* sense, the *auditory* and *kinesthetic* senses are especially important in officiating. The auditory sense refers to sound, such as hearing the game-ending buzzer above the roar of the home-team crowd. The kinesthetic sense is the feel or sensation of the body as it moves in different positions, such as the feeling of different arm positions to signal certain calls.

The emotions associated with various officiating experiences are also important in the practice of imagery. Recreating emotions such as anxiety, anger, joy, or pain through imagery can help control these same emotions. You should try to recreate the feelings you experienced during a game to better understand how your emotions affect your performance.

HOW IMAGERY WORKS

The real mystery surrounding imagery is how it works. Research has provided only limited evidence for why imagery is such a powerful tool in enhancing performance. Sport psychologists have advanced two explanations to account for the imagery-performance phenomenon.

Neuromuscular Facilitation Theory

One explanation holds that vividly imagined events produce activity in the muscles similar to that produced by physically performing the movement. That is, the brain does not distinguish between something that actually happens and something that is vividly imagined. Numerous studies[2,3] involving athletes have demonstrated that, regardless of whether they actually perform movements or vividly imagine performing them, similar nerve pathways to the muscles are used. Of course the muscle and nerve activity is not as great as when the skill is actually performed, but through imagery you can help strengthen the neural pathways for that skill.

Symbolic Learning Theory ⋇

A second explanation of how imagery works may be more relevant to you as an official. This explanation suggests that you learn skills by becoming more familiar with what needs to be done to success-fully perform them. In essence, performers establish a mental blueprint for successfully completing the desired action. Thus imagery facilitates performance by blueprinting or coding actions into symbols that make actions more familiar and perhaps more automatic.

But whether imagery serves to strengthen significant motor path-ways or to make actions more automatic, one thing is certain—it works. So let's look at three ways imagery can help you be a more effective official.

USES OF IMAGERY

You can use imagery to enhance more than just the physical aspect of one officiating performance. Imagery can also help in the following ways: ⋇

- Controls emotional responses
- Improves concentration
- Builds confidence
- Strengthens and corrects performance

Controls Emotional Responses

Officials oftentimes let their anxiety and anger get the best of them during a game. If coaches, players, or fans are rude or abusive, it is easy to lose your cool and act inappropriately. In your role, however, you must maintain your composure and act professionally. Visualization helps you picture provoking situations and then allows you to see your-self keeping under control and dealing with the problem positively.

Improves Concentration

Imagery improves concentration, especially when you are preparing for an upcoming assignment. By visualizing what you want to do and how you want to react, you can prevent your mind from wandering. In addition, you can image yourself in situations when you sometimes lose your concentration (e.g., hostile crowd reactions) and instead see yourself maintaining your composure and refocusing on the action of the performers.

Builds Confidence

One of the ways for an official to build confidence is to officiate lots of games. Besides gaining experience, you can also build self-confidence through the use of imagery. For example, if your confidence is shaken when the crowd starts booing you for calls you've made, then picture a number of these situations. See yourself taking control and maintaining your confidence and impartiality on subsequent calls. When you see yourself doing something well in your mind it will give you confidence that you can in fact perform under adverse circumstances.

Strengthens and Corrects Performance

Imagery is a valuable tool for correcting errors and strengthening the skills you already perform well. Because you'll rarely get to physically practice your craft in a noncompetitive situation, it is even more important that you use imagery to build upon strengths and perfect skills. Some individuals only use imagery when they have a problem such as loss of concentration, indecisiveness, or poor positioning. However, imagery also helps you refine well-learned skills.

TYPES OF IMAGERY

You can assume either an internal or external perspective in your imagery. The perspective you choose will have important implications for the effectiveness of your image.

External Imagery

External imagery involves watching yourself as if you were in a movie or on videotape. From this perspective, your focus is less on actually performing the activity and more on watching yourself do it from a distance. For example, if you were visualizing yourself making a close call at home plate, you would see not only the runner, catcher, home plate, and the ball, but also your back and the back of your head, just as a spectator might.

✓ Internal Imagery

Internal imagery refers to imagining yourself performing from your own eyes. You see what you would ordinarily see when performing the particular action. It would look as if a camera were on your head taking pictures of everything you would see in a given situation. To use the previous example, you would see the ball, the runner, home plate, and the catcher, but you would not see your back or the back of your head.

Comparing Internal and External Imagery

Several studies of imagery[4,5] have indicated that an internal perspective is more beneficial than an external perspective. This is primarily because internal imagery enables you to experience the feelings that occur while performing a given action. Furthermore, the electrical activity in the muscles performing the skill is greater when imaging from an internal perspective. This muscle activity helps to make the imagined skill more automatic during actual performance. A drawback to relying on internal imagery is a lack of objectivity. You aren't given the opportunity to see yourself from an observer's point of view. This can result in missing something important that is out of your line of vision.

The best way to overcome this drawback is to use a combination of external and internal imagery. If you, like some individuals, have trouble generating an internal image, it is quite appropriate to use external imagery. In fact, several research studies have found external imagery to be equally as effective as internal imagery.[6,7] As long as your image is clear, controllable, and detailed, it will be effective.

You also might consider switching back and forth from internal to external imagery, depending on the particular situation or skill that you are working on. This will allow you to experience the benefits of imaging as if you were a performer (internal) and an observer (external).

EVALUATING YOUR IMAGERY

Having been introduced to imagery and its potential uses, you can now consider developing an imagery training program of your very own. The first step is to evaluate your current imagery skill level. We have emphasized that imagery, like other psychological techniques, is a skill that can be learned only through practice. Some of you may have used imagery successfully in the past; some of you will catch on fast, and some of you may have trouble even developing an image in your mind.

You can use a test developed by Martens[8] to evaluate your imagery skills (Self-Help Test 8.1). This inventory measures how well you can use all your senses while imaging. Follow the instructions and do the best that you can. There are no right or wrong answers, and the evaluation should take no more than 15 minutes.

Self-Help Test 8.1
Sporting Official Imagery Questionnaire

As you complete this questionnaire, remember that imagery involves more than just seeing something in your mind. Vivid images include not only visualizing but experiencing all the senses—seeing, hearing, feeling, tasting, and smelling. Along with these sensations you may also experience emotions, moods, or certain states of mind.

In this test, you will read descriptions of four general sport situations. You are to imagine the general situation and provide as much detail from your imagination as possible to make the image as real as you can. Then you will be asked to rate your imagery on four dimensions:

1. How vividly you saw or visualized the image
2. How clearly you heard the sounds
3. How vividly you felt your body movements (kinesthetic sense) during the activity
4. How clearly you were aware of your state of mind or felt the emotions of the situation

(Cont.)

Self-Help Test 8.1 (Continued)

After you read each general description, think of a specific example of it (e.g., the skill, the people involved, the place, the time). Next, close your eyes and take a few deep breaths to become as relaxed as you can. Put aside all other thoughts for a moment. Keep your eyes closed for about one minute as you try to imagine the situation as vividly as you can.

Use your imagery skills to develop a vivid and clear image of the general described situation. Your accurate appraisal of your images will help you to determine which exercise you will want to emphasize in the basic training exercises.

After you have imagined the described situation, please rate the four dimensions of imagery by circling the number that best describes the image you had.

1 = *no image present*
2 = *not clear or vivid, but a recognizable image*
3 = *moderately clear and vivid image*
4 = *clear and vivid image*
5 = *extremely clear and vivid image*

PRACTICING

Select one specific situation or call in the sport you typically officiate such as calling a close play at home in baseball, calling a block or charge in basketball, calling a pass interference in football, or calling a tripping penalty in hockey. Now imagine yourself making this call in a practice situation such as at umpire school or at a clinic or workshop. Close your eyes for about one minute and try to see yourself in this place, hear the sounds, feel your body perform the movement, and be aware of your state of mind or mood.

a. Rate how well you see yourself doing this activity.	1	2	3	4	5
b. Rate how well you hear the sounds of doing the activity.	1	2	3	4	5
c. Rate how well you feel yourself making the movements.	1	2	3	4	5
d. Rate how well you are aware of your mood.	1	2	3	4	5

WATCHING ANOTHER OFFICIAL

Think of another official (maybe someone you've worked with in the past) making a tough call in a critical situation. Close your eyes for about one minute to imagine as vividly and realistically as possible watching your fellow official making that tough call in a crucial situation.

a. Rate how well you saw your fellow official in this situation.	1	2	3	4	5
b. Rate how well you heard the sounds in this situation.	1	2	3	4	5

c. Rate how well you felt your own physical presence or movement in this situation. 1 2 3 4 5

d. Rate how well you felt the emotions of this situation. 1 2 3 4 5

OFFICIATING A GAME

Imagine yourself officiating in an actual game situation. Imagine yourself having to make a difficult call but you are in proper position and you make the call decisively and without hesitation. You feel good that you were right on top of the action and made a good call. Now close your eyes for about one minute and imagine this situation as vividly as possible.

a. Rate how well you saw yourself in this situation. 1 2 3 4 5

b. Rate how well you heard the sounds in this situation. 1 2 3 4 5

c. Rate how well you felt yourself making the movements. 1 2 3 4 5

d. Rate how well you felt the emotions of the situation. 1 2 3 4 5

SCORING

Now let's determine your imagery scores and see what they mean. First, sum the ratings for your three answers to Part "a" in each section, your three answers to Part "b" in each section, and so on, recording them in the proper place below.

Dimension				Total Score
a. Visual	_____	+ _____	+ _____	= _____
b. Auditory	_____	+ _____	+ _____	= _____
c. Kinesthetic	_____	+ _____	+ _____	= _____
d. Mood	_____	+ _____	+ _____	= _____

On a given dimension your top score could be 15 (all 5s) with your lowest score being 3. The closer you came to 15 on each dimension the more skilled you are in that particular area. Lower scores mean that you need to work on those aspects of your imagery.

DEVELOPING YOUR IMAGERY PROGRAM

Regardless of your score on the Sport Imagery Questionnaire, you will need to follow a systematic imagery training program to improve your imagery skills. The program need not be complex or cumbersome but should fit nicely into your daily routine. Evaluate your questionnaire results to pinpoint specific areas in which you need practice.

In this section we'll provide you with tips, guidelines, and suggestions for implementing an imagery training program. It is important to remember that the imagery program you devise must be compatible with your individual needs, abilities, and interests as an official. Then pick out other areas to work on that relate to your officiating situation. And remember, start out slowly. As you become more comfortable with, and skilled at, practicing imagery, add other things to your program.

The basic elements of a successful imagery training program include the following:

- Proper setting
- Relaxed concentration
- Realistic expectations
- Sufficient motivation
- Vivid images
- Controlled images
- Videotaped performances
- Positive focus

Proper Setting

Those highly skilled in the use of imagery can practice and perform the technique in almost any setting. Because few of us possess this skill, it's best to initially practice imagery in a setting that has no distractions.

Some people like to practice imagery in their rooms before going to sleep, whereas others use imagery in the locker room before the event. As you develop your skills, you will learn to use imagery in the face of distractions and even during breaks in the action.

Relaxed Concentration

In chapter 6 you learned several different techniques for relaxation. Research has found that imagery preceded by relaxation is more effective than imagery alone.[9] So prior to every imagery session, get relaxed by using deep breathing, progressive relaxation, or some other relaxation procedure that is effective for you.

Relaxation is important for two reasons. First, by relaxing you can temporarily forget daily hassles and worries and focus your attention on officiating an upcoming game. Second, when your body is physically tense or active, relaxation keeps you from focusing on what's going on inside you. With a quiet state of relaxed concentration, your mind and body can effectively focus on the image you create.

Realistic Expectations and Sufficient Motivation

Individuals can often greatly improve their imagery skills in a few weeks because these skills are typically underdeveloped. In fact, individuals starting an imagery program often expect imagery to result in immediate and continual performance improvements. After the initial spurt, however, progress levels off as it usually does when learning any new skill. We don't want to mislead you; imagery won't work miracles, but it is an effective tool to enhance performance when used properly.

Some individuals refuse to believe that imagery can help them perform better. They subscribe to the notion that hard physical practice is the only way to achieve success. Thus, many individuals either never try to image or enter into an imagery program with great skepticism. They practice infrequently, and, when they do practice, their concentration is poor.

If imagery is to be effective, you must develop your imagery skills in a regular and systematic fashion. This requires dedication and a belief that your imagery program will pay off in terms of making you a more competent official. Imagery requires the same degree of motivation as learning the rules, understanding proper positioning, and getting in top physical condition. They all take a great deal of practice, time, and energy with the expectation that your effort will be rewarded in the future.

Vivid Images

The closer your images are to the real thing, the better they'll transfer to actual performance. Good imagers use all of their senses and try to make their images as vivid and detailed as possible. That is why it is important to hear, see, and feel the situation imagined as accurately as possible. Pay particular attention to environmental details such as the layout of the facilities and the positioning of fences and bleachers.

In addition, experience the emotions and thoughts of the actual officiating situations. Feel the anxiety, concentration, frustration, or anger associated with your performance. This, too, will help make the performance more real. Remember, the more vivid your imagery in terms of using all your senses, the more difficult it is for the body to tell the difference between real and vividly imagined experiences.

If you have trouble getting clear, vivid images, you might first try to imagine things that are very familiar to you, such as the furniture in your house or the office where you work. As you get better at visualizing common things, try to picture yourself officiating a game.

A good setting for nurturing real-life images is in an arena or field where you have officiated before. Here, you will be familiar with the playing surface, grandstands, background, colors, and other environmental details. Then, recall a time when you officiated a game in which you felt you did a particularly exceptional job. Attempt to get a clear picture of the way you moved, the feelings of confidence and control you felt, how your body felt, and what your thoughts and emotions were at the time.

Practice getting vivid images with exercises such as this and the three exercises that follow. We also recommend that you obtain a copy of *Put Your Mother on the Ceiling* by Richard DeMille[10] and try its variety of exercises to further develop the vividness of your imagery.

Exercise 1: Imaging Home

Imagine that you are at home in your living room. Look around and take in all the details. What do you see? Notice the shape and texture of the furniture. What sounds do you hear? Really be there, looking out. What is the temperature like? Is there any movement in the air? What odors do you smell? Use all your senses to take it all in.

Exercise 2: Imaging a Positive Instance

Select a particular officiating situation or call and visualize yourself performing perfectly. It might be calling a very close play, dealing with an irate player or coach, getting into proper position, communicating effectively with your fellow official, or dealing with a hostile crowd. In any case, make sure that you get a clear picture of the situation you are imaging. Notice the colors of the players' uniforms, the faces of the players and coaches, the layout of the playing field, and any other relevant information. Feel your body position as you get into position to make the call. Hear the sounds that typically accompany this situation.

✓Exercise 3: Imaging a Positive Game

Recall as vividly as possible a game when you officiated very well. If you can recall a "finest hour" in recent memory, use that. Your visualization will cover three specific areas of recall: visual, auditory, and kinesthetic.

Your visual recall should recreate a picture of how you look when you're performing well. You should notice that your appearance when you're in control is different from that when you are unsure of yourself; you walk differently; you carry your head and shoulders differently. When you are confident on the inside, it shows on the outside. Try to get as clear a picture as possible of what you look like when you're performing well. Review films of successful performances to help crystallize this image.

For auditory recall, reproduce in your mind the sounds you hear when you are officiating particularly well. Especially listen to the inner dialogue you have with yourself. What is your internal dialogue like? What are you saying to yourself and how are you saying it? What is your internal response when faced with adversity during a game? Recreate all the sounds as vividly as possible.

Your kinesthetic recall should provide clear feelings in your mind of all the bodily sensations you have when you are officiating well. How do your hands and feet feel? Do you have a feeling of looseness or intensity in your body? Do your muscles feel tight or relaxed? Do your movements feel quick or sluggish? Allow the bodily sensations that are associated with your best officiating performances to take over.

Controlled Images

Another key to successful imagery is learning to manipulate or control your images so that they do what you want them to do. Many people have trouble controlling their images, often repeating the same mistakes over and over in their mind. For example, some officials have reported that, when using imagery, they sometimes see themselves making the wrong call again and again. Work at controlling the imagined situation. See yourself making the right decisions with confidence. This is the kind of picture you want to recreate in your mind.

If you are having difficulty controlling your images, start with some very simple everyday tasks such as doing household chores, taking a walk, reading a book, or writing a letter. Practice with these familiar tasks to develop your ability to control images. Then you'll be better prepared to imagine more complex tasks related to officiating.

When you're ready to begin visualizing your officiating performance, set up a specific situation and try to devise an appropriate strategy for dealing with it. For example, you might visualize yourself maintaining your composure and handling an unruly coach in a congenial, yet assertive, manner without losing control of your temper. The key is to be in control of what you visualize. We suggest a couple of exercises that will help you learn to control your images.

Exercise 1: Controlling a Difficult Situation

Imagine yourself working on a specific officiating situation that has given you trouble in the past. Take careful notice of what you were doing wrong. Now imagine yourself handling that situation perfectly. See, hear, and feel your response. Do the same thing for other situations that have also caused you problems. Always try to have the image do what you want it to do.

Exercise 2: Controlling a Difficult Player

Picture yourself officiating a game in which a particular player has given you a hard time in the past. Try to recreate the specific situations in which the player has argued with you. Set up a strategy in your mind for dealing effectively with this player and carry this strategy out in your imagery. Make sure that you stay in control of the situation. See yourself acting in a calm, yet firm, manner.

Videotaped Performances

One problem in trying to improve officiating skill is that you usually can't see what things you're doing right or wrong. That's why it helps to have an instructor or colleague give you feedback about your officiating performance. However, it's also helpful to actually observe yourself on film to have a better idea of how you perform as an official. Then you could actually see your mistakes and have a prototype to recreate your successes.

One way to accomplish this is through the use of videotape. So, if possible, have someone videotape you while you are working a game. This will allow you to develop more vivid images and make you more keenly aware of what you are doing well and where you could use some improvement.

A new program called Sybervision is one example of how technology can be used to enhance images and subsequent performance. Specifically, Sybervision videotapes professionals from different sports (e.g., Stan Smith, tennis; Al Geiberger, golf) who demonstrate perfect (or at least near perfect) form in executing the skills specific to that sport. Less skilled athletes then observe this taped performance a number of times, until it is entrenched in the mind.

You can accomplish the same thing by viewing a videotape of a top official. After the picture of correct performance is established, substitute yourself for the tape's model. Then, replay in your mind yourself successfully executing the skills required to officiate your sport.

Positive Focus

Generally, you should focus on a successful performance when you practice imagery. For instance, see yourself assuming the right position to make a close call or handling an irate coach in a fair, assertive manner.

It is also beneficial to use imagery to improve your self-awareness. This includes recognizing both the good calls and the mistakes you make. And as an official you'll make mistakes just as athletes make errors throughout the course of a game. When you do make a mistake, however, you need to leave the call behind and refocus your attention on the action (chapter 7). Through imagery training you can work on effectively coping with certain mistakes you make frequently.

The point is that visualizing successful outcomes programs the body and mind to execute these skills during the actual game. But because errors and mistakes are also part of being an official, you should be equally prepared to deal effectively with these situations. Imagery is the perfect tool for learning how to cope effectively with errors in your performance.

WHEN TO USE IMAGERY

One of the most often asked questions concerns when to use imagery. Although you can practice imagery at virtually any time, these are some specific times when it is most useful:

- Before and after events
- During breaks in the action
- During personal time

Before and After Events

Imagery is a good way to get your mind focused on the upcoming competition. This allows you to go over in your mind exactly how you want to officiate the contest, thus preparing yourself for different situations. Imagery before a contest helps fine-tune your actions and reactions.

The precise time to use imagery before a contest will depend on the individual. Some officials like to visualize right before the start of the competition, whereas others like to image an hour or two prior to starting. The important point is that imagery should fit comfortably into your pre-event routine. You might even use imagery at two or three different times, such as 2 hours, 1 hour, and 30 minutes before the event. These sessions should be about 10 minutes in length; it is difficult to concentrate on an image for a longer period of time.

Officials often overlook using imagery right after an event. With the competition clearly in your mind, you can replay the calls and situations you dealt with effectively. In addition, you can replay any calls or reactions you were not satisfied with and then image yourself confidently and decisively handling the situation.

During Breaks in the Action

Most sporting events have some extended breaks in the action between periods or quarters or during a half. These break times afford you the chance to use imagery and get ready for what's ahead.

Try to find the least noisy spot where you can relax and visualize without distractions. Reflect on what has occurred and imagine situations that are likely to occur when play resumes. See yourself handling these situations effectively and confidently. This will also help you keep your concentration focused on the job you have yet to accomplish.

During Personal Time

Besides using imagery before, during, and after a competition, you can also use imagery at home (or any other appropriate quiet place). Try to set aside 10 minutes at a particular time of the day so that imagery becomes part of your daily routine. Some individuals like to image just before they go to sleep, whereas others prefer to practice imagery when they wake in the morning. Again, the important point is to have a set time every day (or as often as possible) for imagery so that you can practice it regularly without interruption.

SUMMARY

The psychological skill of imagery is a powerful technique for improving officiating skills. Imagery should involve several senses, allowing you to see, hear, and feel yourself in the situation. Imagery is not magic; rather it works through facilitation of nerve pathways.

Imagery benefits your officiating by controlling emotional responses, improving concentration, building confidence, and improving technique and positioning. You can practice imagery from an internal or an external perspective; the most important thing is to make your images vivid and controllable.

This chapter provides guidelines for implementing an imagery program, but remember that the best imagery program is one that is tailored to your particular needs. If you design an effective imagery program and practice imagery regularly, you'll be a more effective official in the future.

PART V

Staying With It

Burnout
9

Throughout the book we have addressed the numerous psychological skills that officiating requires. You must be able to deal with pressure, maintain concentration, be mentally prepared for the assignment, feel confident and in control, effectively communicate with players and other officials, and stay motivated to officiate effectively, season after season. In addition to coping mentally and physically, officials must juggle family, business, legal, and lifestyle concerns. It is no wonder, then, that many officials burn out.

DEFINITION AND DANGERS OF BURNOUT

As an official, you have to deal with media criticism, irate coaches, hostile crowds, disgruntled athletes, and never-ending pressure to make the right call. If you don't handle these constant pressures properly, they can lead to burnout.

The term *burnout* is used loosely these days, so we'll try to clarify exactly what it means. Burnout involves withdrawing from an activity that at one time was intrinsically interesting but is now boring, unfulfilling, or too demanding. Burnout is characterized as a progressive loss of one's energy, idealism, and purpose. It is a feeling of being locked into a routine, job, or lifestyle that is no longer exciting or pleasurable. This is typically accompanied by feelings of physical and emotional exhaustion and the development of negative attitudes toward your job, your family, yourself, and life in general.

In chapter 6 we discussed some of the causes of anxiety for officials and how anxiety negatively affects performance and offered strategies for coping with anxiety. Perhaps a larger issue is the potential effect of chronic stress on officials. Officials often find that their initial desire to stay involved in sport is diminished by the stressors and demands of the job. A recent study[1] found that fear of failure, role conflict, and other evaluative aspects of officiating were related to burnout. In addition, several anecdotal reports by officials indicate that such chronic stress leads not only to burnout, but to stress-related illnesses.

Here's how a high school basketball and football official described the chronic stress he experienced and its consequence:

> Oftentimes in the middle of a game I'd think to myself, What am I doing here? These guys are going to eat me alive. The frustrations, abuse, and hassles sort of wear on you. It actually caused me to leave officiating for awhile because it started affecting my health.

Unfortunately, the list of officials who have suffered stress-related illnesses is long. Noted professional officials such as Mendy Rudolph, Manny Sokol, Nick Colosi, Don Murphy, and John Kibler all suffered heart attacks at a relatively early age. Some of these attacks actually occurred while they were officiating games.

Many lesser known officials also have suffered physically and psychologically from the stress of officiating. A significant percentage of these officials were simply burned out. So we think it's important that you understand the phenomenon of burnout, know how to identify its symptoms, and are able to take steps to avoid it.

STAGES OF BURNOUT

Most researchers agree that burnout takes time to develop; it doesn't happen overnight. Typically, an individual will pass through a series of stages leading to burnout, although these stages differ depending on the individual's strengths and weaknesses and the particular

environmental demands that he or she might encounter. These four
stages are as follows: ✗ EXPLAIN

1. *Depersonalization*—You begin to dissociate yourself from
   the people you work with as you become emotionally removed, distant, and unconcerned.

2. *Decreased feelings of personal accomplishment*—You start
   to feel that you are no longer making a contribution, that
   you aren't accomplishing what you originally set out to do.
   You no longer gain satisfaction from your job.

3. *Isolation*—You start to isolate and insulate yourself from your
   co-workers. You begin searching for excuses to remove
   yourself from your work setting.

4. *Emotional and physical exhaustion*—You now break down
   emotionally and/or physically. The slow burnout process
   is completed as you have no desire to reenter the workplace
   nor the energy to do so.

SIGNS AND SYMPTOMS OF BURNOUT

People experiencing burnout demonstrate some typical reactions. However, some individuals experiencing the early stages of burnout often don't perceive themselves going through the process. Although they do acknowledge feeling fatigued, bored, or overworked, the burnout candidate is frequently the last person to realize when it's happening. This suggests that an official who is experiencing duress is probably not the best person to evaluate his or her own behavior.

One way for you to identify whether you (or one of your officiating colleagues) are falling victim to burnout is to be aware of its warning signs. Burnout is a complex multidimensional process that may affect you physically, psychologically, behaviorally, or occupationally, and it may affect your family life. Some common burnout reactions under each of these categories are highlighted in Table 9.1. It should be noted that you don't have to be experiencing all of these things to be burned out, nor are you necessarily burned out because you happen to exhibit one or two of these signs. You may be more vulnerable in one area than another. So you'll have to shore up your weakness to prevent burnout. And if you are experiencing several signs or symptoms listed in Table 9.1, you should be especially concerned and take immediate measures to remedy them.

Another way to identify your potential for burnout is by completing Self-Help Test 9.1. This inventory is designed to measure the frequency (how often) and intensity (how strong) of an official's feelings of burnout and is adapted from the Maslach Burnout Inventory.[2] Follow the instructions given at the top of the inventory in reporting how often and strongly you would agree with the 16 statements.

Table 9.1 Signs and Symptoms of Burnout

EXAMPLES

Aspect disrupted	Signs and symptoms
Physical	Headaches, chronic fatigue, decreased fitness, insomnia, ulcer, hypertension
Psychological	Feelings of depression, inappropriate aggression, increased anxiety, increased irritability, loss of temper
Behavioral	Increased rigidity and stubbornness, less efficiency, increased probability of drug use, complaining
Family life	Blurring work and home lives, increased anger, isolation from family, inability to relax
Job reactions	Lower productivity, increased lateness and absenteeism, acceptance of less responsibility

Self-Help Test 9.1
Officiating Burnout

Please read each statement carefully and decide if you ever feel this way about officiating. Select the number (1 to 7) that best describes how frequently you feel this way. Then decide how strong the feeling is when you experience it by selecting the appropriate number (from 1 to 7).

How often	1	2	3	4	5	6	7
	Not often at all						Extremely often

How strong	1	2	3	4	5	6	7
	Not strong at all						Extremely strong

How often 1-7	How strong 1-7	
1. _____	_____	I feel emotionally drained from officiating.
2. _____	_____	I feel fatigued when I get up in the morning and have to face another officiating assignment.
3. _____	_____	I feel I treat players and coaches as if they were impersonal objects.
4. _____	_____	I feel I'm working too hard for too little when I officiate.
5. _____	_____	I accomplish many worthwhile things by officiating.
6. _____	_____	Working with players and coaches is really a strain on me.
7. _____	_____	I feel very energetic.
8. _____	_____	I worry that officiating is hardening me emotionally.
9. _____	_____	I feel frustrated by officiating.
10. _____	_____	Working with undisciplined coaches and players puts too much stress on me.
11. _____	_____	I feel burned out from officiating.
12. _____	_____	I feel I'm positively influencing other people's lives through my officiating.
13. _____	_____	I've become more callous toward people since I started officiating.

(Cont.)

Self Help Test 9.1 (Continued)

	How often 1-7	*How strong 1-7*	
14.	_____	_____	I am totally spent at the end of officiating an event.
15.	_____	_____	I feel like I'm at the end of my rope.
16.	_____	_____	I feel coaches and athletes blame me for most of their problems.

Scoring the test: Items 5, 7, and 12 should be reverse-scored. That is, if you rated item #5 as a 2 on the scale, you would score it as a 6 rating. Add up these three items and the remaining items for both the "How often" and "How strong" columns. Then compare each column score to the rating system for the respective category.

Rating system Frequency of burnout feelings		*Rating system Intensity of burnout feelings*	
Total score	*Burnout status*	*Total score*	*Burnout status*
16-47	Never failing	16-47	High voltage
48-71	Rare malfunctions	48-71	Strong current
72-95	Often on the blink	72-95	Low wattage
96-112	Permanently short-circuited	96-112	Power outage

PREVENTING AND MANAGING BURNOUT

Officiating is a demanding and stressful job; you should take every opportunity to relieve some of the pressure of your work. Although some things might be beyond your control, such as an antagonistic crowd, a difficult assignment, travel hassles, or a baiting coach, *you can control how you deal with these stressors.* By controlling your response to demanding situations, you may prevent your stress level from building and thus never approach burnout.

The five areas that you can address to better cope with stress are

- physical fitness,
- diet,
- mental outlook,
- relaxation, and
- self-regulation.

Stay In Good Physical Condition

Maintaining physical fitness has been recommended in several other parts of this book. This is because the status of your body has much to do with the state of your mind. And the relationship is reciprocal: The state of mind you're in also affects the status of your body. Stress is often manifested in physical illnesses and can lead to or contribute to heart attacks. Staying in shape not only allows you to be a more effective official, but also will make you feel better about yourself and help you fight against the ravages of stress.

Eat Nutritious Foods

Related to staying in shape is watching what you eat. Entire books, such as *Nancy Clark's Sports Nutrition Guidebook*,[3] are devoted specifically to sports nutrition, but some general rules to follow include limiting your salt and sugar intake while getting a proper balance between carbohydrates, fats, and proteins. A well-balanced diet consists of 65% carbohydrates, 20% fats, and 15% protein and is not high in cholesterol.

Keep a Positive Outlook

It is easy to let criticism from the media, coaches, and players get you down. However, you need to continue to focus on the things you do well. Even when you officiate a great game, the losing coach may be upset and try to place the blame on you. Airing your feelings with other officials will help keep your outlook positive while at the same time increasing your social support network.

Take Relaxation Breaks

Try to set aside time to relax as often as possible during the season. Especially on game nights, it's a good idea to get to the game site early so you have time to relax and get yourself ready for the upcoming game. It's also important to wind down after the game and get your mind off work. Don't get consumed by your job and become a workaholic who thinks, eats, and breathes officiating 24 hours a day. It is important to take time off and time away from officiating and enjoy the other aspects of your life. We recommend that you use some of the relaxation techniques discussed in chapter 6.

"It's nice to unwind after a tough game."

Learn Self-Regulation Skills

Throughout the book we have tried to emphasize the importance of developing your psychological skills as they pertain to officiating. You can use many of these self-regulation skills to help ward off the stress that leads to burnout. Imagery, attentional control, self-talk, and goal setting are just some of the self-regulatory techniques you can learn to deal more effectively with the stress of being an official.

Another thing that you can regulate is the number of games you work and the amount of travel that you do. If you work more than one sport you might consider giving up a less enjoyed sport for a season to get reenergized. More is not necessarily better, and fatigue experienced from overwork will hinder your ability and desire to officiate. So try to balance your personal life and officiating schedule reasonably. This not always easy, but it's necessary if you wish to officiate for long.

SUMMARY

Very often the significant stressors that accompany officiating are not dealt with effectively, and thus many officials burn out. In this chapter we described the stages of burnout and suggested how, as an official, you can specifically address these troublesome series of events.

Become more aware of the signs and symptoms of burnout. Unfortunately, many officials do not attend to these signals and before they know it they're no longer officiating; nor are they physically or mentally able to officiate effectively. So, if you start to exhibit some of the typical reactions to chronic stress, stop and see how changing your actions and environment can alleviate these problems.

Special Psychological Influences

10

Your job as an official is an extremely difficult, yet essential, part of sport. We have focused most of the *Psychology of Officiating* on developing the psychological skills necessary to perform effectively in your role. But we have yet to deal with a number of outside influences that can burden you psychologically. You should know how to properly address each of these factors, for they can severely impair your officiating performance—and well-being—if handled inappropriately. Among these important extraneous factors are the following:

- Legal considerations
- Gambling
- Drug use
- Injuries and illnesses

LEGAL CONSIDERATIONS

Competent officials have a good grasp of their sport's rules and know how to apply them. But nowadays, good officials also know their legal responsibilities and how to live up to them.

You don't need a law degree to understand your legal duties as an official. What you do need is a written and signed agreement with the league's management that explicitly states what you can and cannot be held liable for. You should also check the legal guidelines recommended by the major association of officials in your sport.

Knowledge of dos and don'ts won't ensure that your actions will be error-free, but it will allow you to be more confident, less anxious, more decisive, and better focused while calling a game. Remember, these are the qualities that characterize the most competent officials (see chapter 1).

Along with sufficient knowledge of your responsibilities, you must take preventive measures to protect yourself as fully as possible against legal hassles. These measures involve the following:

* Contractual agreements
* Personal liability insurance
* Playing site hazards
* Weather conditions
* Safety guidelines
* Sideline personnel and security
* Player injuries

Contractual Agreements

As in other legal matters, possession of a written legal document provides better protection than handshakes or verbal agreements. Some states require that a written contract be signed by both the school and the officials working the contest. If the state you work in has no such stipulation, construct a formal agreement that, if signed by you and the contest-sponsoring agency, will provide adequate protection.

Such a contract might include the date and site of the game, the fees and expenses to be paid to you, your obligations in terms of times for arrival and departure and job duties, and what recourse either party has if either you or the sponsoring agency fail to live up to the contract.

Personal Liability Insurance

A recreational wrestler was injured when his opponent picked him up and slammed him to the mat. The referee was sued for failure to properly supervise.

No official should be without insurance coverage. An official who doesn't have it is likely to be too cautious and perhaps worried about possibly contributing to a mishap. Insurance coverage will allow you to perform to your full potential, without such inhibiting concerns.

Liability insurance will pay, up to the policy limit, any monetary damages you might be obligated to pay in the event of injury to an athlete participating in an event you're working. In addition, liability insurance can help absorb the cost of legal fees should you require legal counsel. This last point is important, as the cost of defending against lawsuits can be very substantial, even for what seem to be minor cases.

Playing Site Hazards

A high school long jumper injured his leg while performing his event. A track official was sued for negligence for permitting an unsafe take-off board to be used for the field event.

Officials are responsible for determining if the playing area is safe for competition. If you are working with a partner or several associates, you might divide up the playing area prior to the contest and examine each section closely for potential hazards. During this visual inspection, be on the alert for uneven, worn, or slick surface areas; the presence of protruding objects; unsafe equipment; and the misplacement of game-related objects.

Uncertainty over the condition of the playing area or equipment can preocccupy and distract even the best official. So free up your mind to focus on the action by inspecting the site closely prior to and during breaks in the game.

Weather Conditions

A $10 million lawsuit was filed against an official by a mother whose son was struck by lightning and killed during a Little League baseball game.

When officiating an outdoor event, it is the responsibility of the officials to determine if the weather conditions are appropriate for play to begin or to continue once it begins. Several lawsuits have cited officials as negligent for injuries that were allegedly contributed to by weather-related factors. For example, a crew of high school football officials was sued for permitting a game to be played on a muddy field after a player slipped, fractured two vertebrae, and was partially paralyzed in attempting to make a tackle.

If you have any doubts about the safety of the playing surface because of the weather, err on the side of safety. Discuss the situation

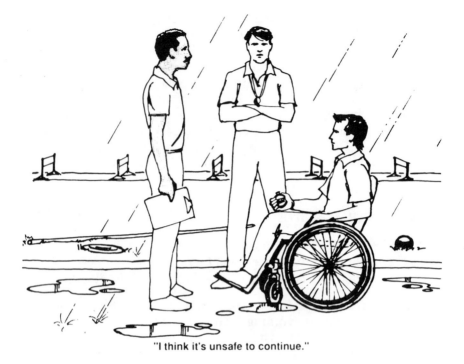

"I think it's unsafe to continue."

with your associates and consider foremost the well-being of the participants. Another consideration should be how the weather will hinder your own ability to perform. For instance, if it is foggy, will you be able to determine whether a long fly ball down the line was fair or foul? Don't put yourself in the position of doubt, for such doubt only leads to anxiety and subsequent performance problems.

Safety Guidelines

A recreational softball player filed a claim against the sports officials' association for failure to properly train and supervise its umpires. The injury allegedly occurred when the player slid into second base, which was improperly tied down, resulting in the spike going through the player's leg.

Many sport rules have been instituted with athletes' safety in mind. For example, players in most sports are prohibited from wearing equipment, casts, or jewelry that might endanger themselves or an opponent. It is up to you to be observant and forbid such articles from being worn by participants in events you officiate. For example, if you failed to notice a ring on a wrestler that accidentally scratched an opponent's eye, you would be held accountable. Therefore, you must stay mentally sharp and be keenly observant. Routinely use self-talk reminders and mental checklists to avoid such slipups.

Sideline Personnel and Security

A high school football player was injured when he was tackled during a game. A claim was filed against the local officials' association for failure to insure that appropriate medical staff was present to attend to the injury.

Sideline observers' function and distance from play are additional legal considerations that you must address. Security and medical personnel should be on hand at every game. If they aren't, you may be put in a position that is beyond your control. You will at least be burdened with yet another concern that can discourage proper attentional focus.

You also must be watchful that nonparticipants are kept at a safe distance from the field of play. Two particularly troublesome sideline groups are photographers and cheerleaders. Both tend to station themselves too near the playing area and put themselves and the athletes in jeopardy of injury. Talk to the media and cheerleading squads prior to the game and designate the boundaries that they must not cross. Note that any violation of these areas will warrant removal from their near-sideline positions. Handling the situation in this manner will prevent problems during the game or at least make more clear-cut your decision when they get too close to the action.

Player Injuries

A junior high school football player injured his neck and back while making a tackle. A lawsuit was filed against two officials for assisting in administering first aid when they were not qualified to do so, and thus aggravating the injuries.

Although it may seem inhumane and unsympathetic, your response to athlete injuries should be one of noninvolvement. That doesn't mean that you should not bring an injury to others' attention or that you should permit an obviously wounded athlete to continue to participate. But it does mean that you should not embark on medical treatments or actions that in any way affect an injured athlete's status.

If you feel assured about your role when injuries occur, you'll be less troubled by the possibility of such incidents and feel less responsible for them. And you'll be less susceptible to lawsuits. So discuss with your officiating associates prior to the game exactly what you will do when injuries occur. We recommend taking these seven steps outlined by Narol:[1]

1. Stop the contest as soon as possible.
2. Report the injury to the player's coach.
3. Report the injury to the game-site administrator (determine prior to the game who this individual is and where he or she will be).
4. Go to a location away from the injured player and remain there.
5. Do not touch, move, or assist in moving the injured player.
6. Do not resume the game until the injured player is pronounced ready to play by the coach or medical personnel or is removed from the playing area.
7. Be patient as you wait for medical personnel to arrive; let them attend to the injured player and determine what measures are required.

GAMBLING

If I fix a game, I want to get an official. They're the first target. If you can't get an official, I try to get a coach. If you can't get a coach, get a kid.[2]

That's the thinking among sport gamblers according to Bob Barrett, former associate commissioner of the Southeastern Conference and former investigator for the Federal Bureau of Investigation for 26 years. Yet rarely do we hear or read about sports officials fixing a game. Why?

One reason is that athletes and coaches have historically received the brunt of media attention in cases involving gambling and point-fixing. From the Black Sox Scandal in 1919 to Pete Rose's removal from major league baseball in 1989, and all of the Art Schlicters (Ohio State football) and John "Hot Rod" Williams (Tulane basketball) in between, the celebrated incidents of sport misconduct have not involved officials.

A second, and more important, reason is that individuals who enter into officiating do so with a commitment to see that the outcome of the event—and the score—is determined solely by the performance of the athletes and coaches. As Jim Delaney, the Big Ten Conference Commissioner says, the best possible safeguard that colleges and professional organizations have against officials' gambling is that officials' first priority is not money, or extra money. Rather, officials are committed to upholding certain principles and seeing that the sport they love is played according to the rules.[3]

Be prepared for questions about your impartiality, even if you had few controversies during the contest. Warren Welsh, director of security for the National Football League, said that his office receives numerous calls every Monday morning from people alleging that officials who worked games the day before were biased in their judgments. He went on to say that each allegation is investigated but none has ever been found to be true.[4]

Integrity is an official's most basic quality (see chapter 1). If administrators, coaches, athletes, or fans have good reason to question your integrity, you'll have a hard time overcoming that reputation. Furthermore, you may begin to doubt your own judgment and become hesitant and inconsistent in your calls. So remain above reproach, as the vast majority of officials do; and "call 'em as you see 'em," not as others suggest that you see 'em.

Guidelines to Discourage Gambling

Here are some commonsense suggestions to ensure that your integrity won't be compromised.

1. Stay away from bars, restaurants, and clubs that have questionable reputations. Bookmakers and gamblers tend to frequent these establishments, so avoid interacting with them by drinking, eating, and socializing elsewhere.
2. Do not answer game-related questions. Any response might be construed as a "tip" for bettors. For example, if you tell a reporter that you intend to call a basketball game closely, it might signal to those betting on the game that the more physical team will be restricted. Thus your best response to questions regarding a specific upcoming game is simply, "No comment."
3. Conduct your personal life in a manner that discourages overtures from gambling types. A FBI agent warned umpires attending a recent training camp that gamblers seek out officials with character flaws as their prey. Then they use this information as leverage to manipulate their subjects. So if you drink a lot or bet on other sporting events, now is the time to stop—before you become the target of those who are searching for an advantage.
4. Maintain complete financial records that are above suspicion. A quick jump in income can raise the eyebrows of league administrators and set you up for unnecessary doubts about its source unless you document it. Also, if gamblers perceive that you are in debt, they may seek to provide a loan that they will expect you to repay with slanted officiating performance. Therefore, keep your finances in order and stay clear of the sharks looking for a piece of you.
5. Exercise caution in all of your public statements. You never know when an off-the-cuff, seemingly innocent remark might be used

as a tip by gamblers. Be cognizant that friendly acquaintances may be more interested in information regarding an upcoming event than they are in establishing a relationship.

DRUG USE

I started drinking and smoking marijuana at age 16. Millions of people do the same thing every day, and I was just one of them.

That's how one official described the behavior that led to his suspension. And it's hard to argue that such behavior is not the norm for many individuals in our drug-addicted society. We have pills to keep us up and pills to put us to sleep, medicines that build muscle and medicines that relax muscle, substances that alter perception of reality and still others that heighten experience of events.

Types of Drugs

The variety and quantity of available drugs are such that it takes an informed and determined effort to avoid abusing them. Drugs can be divided into three categories:

- *Additive*   Drugs that supposedly enhance performance beyond normal capabilities, including anabolic steroids, amphetamines, cocaine, and barbiturates.
- *Restorative*   Drugs that return the body to its normal state. Included among this category are muscle relaxants, pain-killers, and anti-inflammatory drugs.
- *Recreational* Drugs that are used for "fun" socially or pleasure individually. Cigarettes, alcohol, and marijuana represent only a few of these types of drugs.

Officials Using Drugs

Drugs are part of an official's workaday world. They're no big deal if used in moderation.

This official's viewpoint illustrates why it is naive to assume that officials are drug-free in a sporting environment that is too often rife with drugs. While players resort to steroids, coaches to stimulants, and fans to booze, officials obviously will be tempted as well.

Reasons for Using Drugs

In fact, because of the high stress associated with officiating, officials may be even more susceptible than individuals in other vocations. In addition to the self-imposed demands to excel and achieve, officials are burdened with expectations of perfection by coaches, players, fans, and the media. Also, supervisors and administrators closely monitor each performance, catching any flaw that may appear. And to top it off, most officials assume their role only after a day of work at their full-time jobs. Thus it is not surprising that many officials resort to the behavior described by this city recreational league umpire:

> I had a few beers after work before heading to the ballpark. I needed to relax after a hard day at the office.

And it doesn't get any easier when the stakes get higher. As one professional sport official said,

> Officiating isn't all glamor. It is tedious and demanding. It consists of long hours spent traveling and sleeping in hotel rooms. Sometimes it is a dull routine. What harm can a little pill do?

Dangers of Using Drugs

We trust that you are aware of the severe physical implications of drug abuse, and the legal and moral ramifications also should be apparent. But more specifically related to your officiating are these four general performance effects of using drugs:

- Slowed or inappropriate motor responses
- Acute and chronic physiologic reactions
- Impaired cognitive functioning
- Altered emotional states

None of these effects will enhance your performance as an official. Each will hinder your ability to attain the psychological skills described in the previous chapters of this book. For example, the confidence you may feel after taking a drug is only a false and transient form of confidence, not a strong, stable, positive feeling of self that is achieved through officiating accomplishments. But even if a drug did improve a particular aspect of your officiating, the price you would pay for resorting to it is not worth the cost. There is a fine line between additive and addictive drug use.

Take some time to assess the extent of your use of drugs. See if there is a pattern to your drug use. Do you use drugs when you are upset? Is your drug intake higher before or after a game? What drug tends to be most troublesome for you?

If you are on prescribed medications, check to see that the dosage is appropriate. Reduce and then end your reliance on nonessential drugs that can easily be abused. Then, when a fan in the stands hollers "Ref, you're a dope!", you can turn to the individual and say with total honesty and conviction "No, I'm not!"

INJURIES AND ILLNESSES

Injuries and illnesses to sports officials come in many forms. Although we have a tendency to think about them in physical terms, psychological problems are at least as likely to strike. And it is very common for psychological and physical ailments to accompany or precipitate one another.

Game Injuries

One of your primary responsibilities as an official is to protect the players. Skillful and effective officials prevent injuries and unnecessary accidents for players; but in the course of doing so, they often put

themselves in precarious positions. In fact, an official who steps between players to break up a fight sometimes emerges from the altercation with more damage than the participating athletes.

In-game injuries do not occur frequently, but they should not be viewed as unique either. A hockey official will sometimes be slammed against the boards, a football official will get crushed by blitzing linebackers, a tennis official may get struck by an 80-mph serve, and a baseball umpire will get hit by pitches. These events not only cause physical pain, but also produce fear and anxiety. Such mishaps might cause you to focus attention on potential injury rather than the contest, thus reducing your effectiveness. To control anxiety and build confidence, follow these simple suggestions:

1. Recognize and understand that potential game injuries are more pronounced in sports in which the official is active rather than passive (e.g., wrestling referee vs. gymnastics judge).
2. Remind yourself during dead spots in the game about basic positions and think of the alternative movements of players. Study player and team tendencies so you can avoid getting in the way.
3. Stay alert with self-talk. All it takes is 1 second of mental letdown to get caught in a position that exposes you to injury.

Postgame Injuries

Physical assaults on sports officials increased during the late 1970s and early 1980s. We witnessed an attack by an irate father on referees who had a penalty called on his son as they left the field after a Midget league football game (ages 9-11). We have seen irrational fans stream on the court after a volleyball game to get even with the officials who "stole" the game from them. We have observed a boxing referee in the 1988 Olympic Games being grabbed and pushed by disgruntled fans and team managers and requiring protection to reach the locker room.

Yes, as an official you'll need to be prepared to be the scapegoat for unfavorable outcomes of athletic contests. If you aren't, the fans, coaches, and players will intimidate you and have a profound impact on your psyche.

These psychological injuries may be more difficult to detect than physical injuries because they affect self-esteem and self-confidence. However, psychological injuries leave internal scars that can be manifested as self-doubt, indecisiveness, negative thinking, and anger. Such injuries, as you might guess, lead to less than optimal officiating performance.

Illness

Medical researchers have established a definite link between physical and psychological stress and a host of physical diseases. For example, stress is related to heart problems, ulcers, high blood pressure, colon difficulties, asthma, and headaches.

Stress-related illnesses are all too real to us and probably to you if you've officiated for any length of time. We have had a professional associate suffer a heart attack on the soccer field and another who blacked out in the locker room after the game. Thus every official must recognize the potential physical and psychological manifestations of an illness.

You must learn to think in preventive terms if you are to have a long officiating career. We offer these physical and psychological health considerations to help you have a productive future as an official:

Physical Considerations

1. Get a physical examination on a regular basis.
2. Stay within your recommended weight range and keep fit.
3. Work the stress out by exercising routinely.
4. Don't abuse your body with drugs, improper diet, or lack of sleep.

Psychological Considerations

1. Take time to relax (have a quiet time for yourself).
2. Develop relaxation or coping skills (see chapters 6 and 8).
3. Adjust officiating goals to meet your needs.
4. Know when to hang up the whistle.

SUMMARY

As an official you have to deal with psychological influences that call upon more than game-related skills. For example, you'll encounter legal, gambling, and drug issues with which you must cope. Injuries and illnesses are additional factors that could limit your ability to officiate. Be aware of how these outside influences can have an impact on your officiating. And employ the coping strategies outlined in this chapter in combination with the psychological skills described in the preceding parts of the book to effectively handle the psychologically demanding job of officiating.

APPENDIX A

Specific Instructions for Progressive Relaxation

In each step you will be asked to first tense a muscle group and then relax it. You need to pay close attention to how it feels to be relaxed as opposed to tense. The tension phase should last 5 to 7 seconds, as will the relaxation phase. Repeat this tension-relaxation cycle twice for each muscle group before moving on to the next group. As you become more skillful you can omit the tension phase and focus just on relaxation. It is usually a good idea to put the following instructions on tape; you might even invest a few dollars in one of the progressive relaxation tapes on the market.

Get as comfortable as possible. Loosen any tight-fitting clothing and do not have your legs crossed. Take a deep breath, let it out slowly, and become as relaxed as possible. When you feel calm and your breathing is slow and regular you are ready to begin.

1. Raise your arms and extend them in front of you.
   - Now make a fist with both hands as tightly as you can.
   - Notice the uncomfortable tension in your hands and fingers.
   - Hold the tension for 5 seconds, then let the tension out halfway and hold for an additional 5 seconds.
   - Then let your hands relax completely.
   - Notice how the tension and discomfort drain from your hands and are replaced by sensations of comfort and relaxation.
   - Focus on the contrast between the tension you felt and the relaxation you now feel.
   - Concentrate on relaxing your hands completely for 10 to 15 seconds.

2. Tense your upper arm hard for 5 seconds.
   - Focus on the feeling of tension.
   - Then let the tension out halfway and hold for an additional 5 seconds.
   - Again focus on the tension that is still present.
   - Now relax your upper arms completely for 10 to 15 seconds and focus carefully on the developing relaxation.
   - Let your arms rest limply at your sides.

3. Wrinkle your forehead and scalp as tightly as possible.
   - Hold the tension for 5 seconds, and then release halfway and hold for another 5 seconds.
   - Relax your scalp and forehead completely.
   - Focus on the developing feeling of relaxation and contrast it with the tension that existed earlier.
   - Concentrate for about a minute on relaxing all of the muscles of your body.

4. Clench your teeth and notice the tension in the muscles of your jaw.
   - After 5 seconds, let the tension out halfway and hold for 5 seconds, and then relax completely.
   - Let your mouth and facial muscles relax completely with your lips slightly parted, and concentrate on totally relaxing these muscles for 10 to 15 seconds.

5. While keeping the muscles of your torso, arms, and legs relaxed, tense your neck muscles by bringing your head forward until your chin digs into your chest.
   - Hold for 5 seconds, release the tension halfway and hold for another 5 seconds, and then relax your neck completely.
   - Allow your head to hang comfortably while you focus on the relaxation developing in your neck muscles.

6. Press the palms of your hands together and push to tense the chest and shoulder muscles.
   - Hold the tension for 5 seconds, then let the tension out halfway and hold for an additional 5 seconds.
   - Now relax the muscles completely and concentrate on the relaxation until your muscles are completely loose and relaxed.
   - Concentrate also on the muscle groups that have been previously relaxed.

7. Move your shoulders back as far as possible until your shoulder blades come close together to tense your back muscles.
   - Let the tension out halfway after 5 seconds, hold the reduced tension, and focus on it carefully for an additional 5 seconds.
   - Relax your back and shoulder muscles completely.
   - Focus on the relaxation as it spreads across the back and shoulder area.

8. Tense your stomach muscles as tightly as possible for 5 seconds and concentrate on the tension.
   - Then let the tension out halfway and hold for an additional 5 seconds before relaxing your stomach muscles completely.
   - Focus on the spreading relaxation until your stomach muscles are completely relaxed.

9. Extend your legs, raise them approximately 6 inches above the floor, and tense your thigh muscles.

   • Hold the tension for 5 seconds, let it out halfway and hold for an additional 5 seconds, and then relax your thighs completely.
   • Concentrate on totally relaxing your feet, calves, and thighs for about 30 seconds.

10. Point your toes away from you and tense your feet and calves.

    • Hold the tension tightly for 5 seconds, let it out halfway and hold for an additional 5 seconds.
    • Relax your feet and calves completely for 10 to 15 seconds.

11. Curl your toes as tightly as possible.

    • After 5 seconds relax the toes halfway and hold the reduced tension for an additional 5 seconds.
    • Then relax your toes completely and focus on the relaxation spreading into the toes.
    • Continue relaxing your toes for 10 to 15 seconds.

Cue-controlled relaxation is the final goal of progressive relaxation. Breathing can serve as the impetus and cue for bringing about feelings of relaxation. The efficiency and ease of the relaxation technique will allow you to apply it during breaks in games. However, this skill is difficult to master. So you must practice the progressive relaxation procedure regularly and work at improving your ability to relax.

When you are able to relax with little difficulty, try this cue-controlled method of relaxation.

   • Take a series of short inhalations, about one a second, until the chest is filled.
   • Hold for about 5 seconds, then exhale slowly for about 10 seconds while thinking to yourself the word ''relax'' or ''calm.''
   • Repeat the process at least five times, each time striving to deepen the state of relaxation that you're experiencing.

APPENDIX B

Sports Officials'
Bill of Rights

1. *Sports Officials shall receive game assignments without regard to sex, race, age, national origin, religion, or any other factor unrelated to ability to perform officiating duties.*

2. *Sports Officials shall be entitled to a written contract for each game assignment delineating their rights and obligations and those of the contracting institution.*

3. *Sports Officials shall be accorded by the host site full security and protection from physical assaults from the time of arrival at the site through time of departure.*

4. *Sports Officials shall be accorded by the host site full security for their personal property they bring with them to the site.*

5. *Sports Officials shall not be responsible for player injuries, except when caused by proven gross negligence.*

6. *Sports Officials' game decisions shall not be subject to administrative or judicial review, except where there is an allegation of fraud, curruption, or abuse of position.*

7. *Sports Officials' civil rights shall not be abridged.*

8. *Sports Officials shall have the right to make a free and voluntary choice as to associations desired to be joined.*

9. *Sports Officials shall be entitled to a due process hearing and appeal when subject to any disciplinary or termination proceedings by an association or league.*

10. *Sports Officials shall be indemnified by the contracting institution for any claims for negligence brought against them arising out of their officiating duties.*

References

Chapter 1

1. Snyder, E.E., & Purdy, D.A. (1987). Social control in sport: An analysis of basketball officiating. *Sociology of Sport Journal*, **4**, 394-402.
2. Snyder, E.E., & Purdy, D.A. (1987). Social control in sport: An analysis of basketball officiating. *Sociology of Sport Journal*, **4**, 394-402.
3. Luciano, R., & Fisher, D. (1982). *The umpire strikes back*. New York: Bantam.

Chapter 2

1. Lawson, R. (1976, September/October). Do you have enough wind to blow your whistle? *Referee*, pp. 33-37.
2. Clegg, R., & Thompson, W.A. (1979). *Modern sports officiating*. Dubuque, IA: William C. Brown.
3. Casada, J. (1986, September). My pet peeves about officials. *Referee*, p. 68.
4. Tapp, J. (1985, May). What do coaches look for in officials? *Referee*, pp. 56-57.
5. Magill, R. (1989). *Motor learning: Concepts and applications*. Dubuque, IA: William C. Brown.

Chapter 3

1. Hall, E.T. (1966). *The hidden dimension*. New York: Doubleday.
2. Snyder, E.E., & Purdy, D.A. (1987). Social control in sport: An analysis of basketball officiating. *Sociology of Sport Journal*, **4**, 394-402.
3. Mano, B. (1986, October). Referee checklist. *Referee*, p. 58.
4. Hill, M.B. (1986, May). Crews. *Referee*, pp. 53-56.
5. Hill, M.B. (1986, May). Crews. *Referee*, pp. 53-56.

Chapter 4

1. Gould, D., Weiss, M., & Weinberg, R. (1981). Psychological characteristics of successful and nonsuccessful Big Ten wrestlers. *Journal of Sport Psychology*, **3**, 69-81.
2. Highlen, P.S., & Bennett, B.B. (1979). Psychological characteristics of successful and nonsuccessful elite wrestlers: An exploratory study. *Journal of Sport Psychology*, **1**, 123-137.

3. Weinberg, R., Gould, D., & Jackson, A. (1979). Expectations and performance: An empirical test of Bandura's self-efficacy theory. *Journal of Sport Psychology*, **1**, 320-331.
4. Weinberg, R., Gould, D., Yukelson, D., & Jackson, A. (1981). The effects of preexisting and manipulated self-efficacy on a competitive muscular endurance task. *Journal of Sport Psychology*, **4**, 345-354.
5. Feltz, D., Landers, D., & Raeder, U. (1979). Enhancing self-efficacy in high-avoidance motor tasks: A comparison of modeling techniques. *Journal of Sport Psychology*, **1**, 112-122.
6. Bandura, A. (1989). *Social foundations of thought and action: A social cognitive theory*. Englewood Cliffs, NJ: Prentice Hall.

Chapter 5

1. Bell, K. (1983). *Championship thinking*. Englewood Cliffs, NJ: Prentice Hall.
2. Locke, E., Shaw, K., Saari, L., & Latham, G. (1981). Goal setting and task performance: 1969-1980. *Psychological Bulletin*, **90**(1), 125-152.
3. Locke, E., Shaw, K., Saari, L., & Latham, G. (1981). Goal setting and task performance: 1969-1980. *Psychological Bulletin*, **90**(1), 125-152.
4. Locke, E., & Latham, G. (1985). The application of goal setting to sports. *Journal of Sport Psychology*, **7**, 205-222.
5. Furst, D. (1989, June). *Motivation to participate in sports officiating*. Paper presented at the meeting of the North American Society for Sport Psychology and Physical Activity, Kent, OH.

Chapter 6

1. Staff. (1987, November). Interview: Bob Herrold. *Referee*, p. 23.
2. Tunney, J. (1987, July). They said it couldn't be done. *Referee*, p. 26.
3. Kroll, W. (1979). The stress of high performance athletics. In P. Klavora & J. Daniel (Eds.), *Coach, athlete, and sport psychologist* (pp. 211-219). Toronto: University of Toronto.
4. Rotella, R., McGuire, R., & Gansneder, B. (1985). *Stress and basketball officials: Impact on health, performance, and retention*. Unpublished manuscript, University of Virginia, Charlottesville.
5. Rotella, R., McGuire, R., & Gansneder, B. (1985). *Stress and basketball officials: Impact on health, performance, and retention*. Unpublished manuscript, University of Virginia, Charlottesville.
6. Rotella, R., McGuire, R., & Gansneder, B. (1985). *Stress and basketball officials: Impact on health, performance, and retention*. Unpublished manuscript, University of Virginia, Charlottesville.
7. Sonstroem, R., & Bernardo, P. (1982). Intraindividual pregame state anxiety and basketball performance: A re-examination of the inverted-U curve. *Journal of Sport Psychology*, **4**, 235-245.

8. Weinberg, R. (1989). Anxiety, arousal and motor performance: Theory, research, and applications. In D. Hackfort & C.D. Spielberger (Eds.), *Anxiety in sports* (pp. 95-116). New York: Hemisphere Publishing.
9. Martens, R. (1987). *Coaches guide to sport psychology*. Champaign, IL: Human Kinetics.
10. Loehr, J. (1982). *Mental toughness training for sports*. Lexington, MA: Stephen Greene Press.
11. Martens, R. (1987). *Coaches guide to sport psychology*. Champaign, IL: Human Kinetics.
12. Loehr, J. (1982). *Mental toughness training for sports*. Lexington, MA: Stephen Greene Press.
13. Jacobson, E. (1983). *Progressive relaxation*. Chicago: University of Chicago Press.
14. Taylor, A. (1989). *Perceived stress, psychological burnout and paths to turnover among sport officials*. Paper presented at the Annual Conference for Psychomotor Learning and Sport Psychology, Ontario, Canada.

Chapter 7

1. Gauron, E. (1984). *Mental training for peak performance*. Lansing, NY: Sport Science Associates.

Chapter 8

1. Nicklaus, J. (1974). *Golf my way*. New York: Simon and Schuster.
2. Feltz, D., & Landers, D. (1983). The effects of mental practice on motor skill learning and performance. A meta-analysis. *Journal of Sport Psychology*, **5**, 25-57.
3. Suinn, R. (1984). Imagery in sports. In W. Straub, & J. Williams (Eds.), *Cognitive sport psychology* (pp. 252-272). Lansing, NY: Sport Science Associates.
4. Hale, B. (1982). The effects of internal and external imagery on muscular and ocular concomitants. *Journal of Sport Psychology*, **4**, 379-387.
5. Harris, D., & Robinson, W. (1986). The effects of skill level on EMG activity during internal and external imagery. *Journal of Sport Psychology*, **8**, 105-111.
6. Epstein, M.L. (1980). The relationship of mental imagery and mental rehearsal on performance of a motor task. *Journal of Sport Psychology*, **2**, 211-220.
7. Ryan, E.D., & Simons, J. (1982). Efficacy of mental imagery in enhancing mental rehearsal of motor skills. *Journal of Sport Psychology*, **4**, 441-451.

8. Martens, R. (1982). *Imagery in sport*. Paper presented at the Medical and Scientific Aspects of Elitism in Sport Conference, Brisbane, Australia.
9. Weinberg, R., Seabourne, T., & Jackson, A. (1981). Effects of visuo-motor behavior rehearsal, relaxation and imagery on karate performance. *Journal of Sport Psychology*, **3**, 228-238.
10. DeMille, R. (1973). *Put your mother on the ceiling: Children's imagination games*. NY: Viking Press.

Chapter 9

1. Taylor, A.H. (1989). *Perceived stress, psychological burnout and paths to turnover intention among sport officials*. Paper presented at the Annual Conference for the Canadian Society for Psychomotor Learning and Sport Psychology, Ontario, Canada.
2. Maslach, C., & Jackson, S. (1981). The measurement of experienced burnout. *Journal of Occupational Therapy*, **2**, 99-113.
3. Clark, N. (1990). *Nancy Clark's sports nutrition guidebook*. Champaign, IL: Leisure Press.

Chapter 10

1. Narol, M. (1986, February). The official's pre-game checklist. *Referee*, pp. 30-31, 59.
2. Monaghan, P. (1986, February). And lead us not into temptation. *Referee*, p. 53.
3. Monaghan, P. (1986, February). And lead us not into temptation. *Referee*, p. 55.
4. Monaghan, P. (1986, February). And lead us not into temptation. *Referee*, p. 55.

Index

P

Pallone, Dave, 41
Pose, 9-10
Postgame evaluation, 23-24
Pregame preparation
  game strategies and, 15-16, 22
  physical, 16-19
  psychological, 19-23
  routines, 15-16

R

Rapport, 8
Relaxation
  breath control for, 92-94
  mental, 95-100
  on-site tips for, 100-102
  progressive, 94-95, 171-173
  self-talk and, 95-100
Rice, Jerry, 72
Rose, Pete, 41, 162
Rudolph, Mendy, 38, 148
Rush, Ed, 81

S

Schlicter, Art, 162
Self-help test
  burnout, 151-152
  communication, 42-43
  concentration, 117-119
  confidence, 54-56
  imagery, 133-135
Smith, Stan, 141
Socha, David, 72
Sokol, Manny, 148
Springstead, Marty, 72
Strom, Earl, 72, 81

T

Tunney, Jim, 72

V

Vargo, Ed., 5

W

Welsh, Warren, 162
Williams, John "Hot Rod", 162